God
First
Loved
Us

God First Loved Us

The Challenge of Accepting Unconditional Love

by

Antony F. Campbell, S.J.

PAULIST PRESS
New York/Mahwah, N.J.

Cover design by Morris Berman Studio

Library of Congress Cataloging-in-Publication Data

Campbell, Antony F.
  God first loved us : the challenge of accepting unconditional love / by Antony F. Campbell.
    p.   cm.
  ISBN 0-8091-3977-4 (alk. paper)
  1. God—Love. I. Title.

BT140 .C26 2000
231'.6—dc21

00-055739

Distributed in Australia by
Rainbow Book Agencies Pty Ltd
Word of Life Distributors
303 Arthur Street
Fairfield, VIC 3078

Published by Paulist Press
997 Macarthur Boulevard
Mahwah, New Jersey 07430

www.paulistpress.com

Printed and bound in the United States of America

CONTENTS

Carrie

Epigraph

I love thee, O thou Lord most high,
Because thou first hast loved me.
I seek no other liberty
Than that of being bound to thee.
All mine is thine, say but the word;
Whate'er thou willest shall be done.
I know thy love, all gracious Lord;
I know it seeks my good alone.

Rev. Edward Caswall, Oratorian (1814–1878)
St. Ignatius Loyola, Jesuit (1491–1556)

Acknowledgments———

Many people have contributed to the birth of this book. Conscious awareness of God's unconditional love as the core of the Christian message probably surfaced for me around 1980. At a deeper level, it has to go back so much further. It is a topic I have talked about with many people, thrashing out questions of how we can believe God loves us unconditionally, how we can cling to that faith in view of all the suffering in the world, how we can find expression for it that does not strip our lives of their seriousness. There have been many, many conversations about these concerns.

Specific people have been directly involved in the preparation of the text. My gratitude to them is deep; their impact on my text has been considerable. It is appropriate to single out certain faculty and friends: Andrew Bullen, Keith Carley, Patricia Chisholm, Maryanne Confoy, Feliz Gil-Jimenez, Andrew Hamilton, Mark O'Brien, Nicole Rotaru, Carmel Wallis. To them my heartfelt thanks. Morag Fraser is the editor of *Eureka Street*, where the bulk of these reflections first appeared.* I am deeply grateful for the care and sensitivity that she gave to my work. Without her painstaking editorial attention, my text would be greatly diminished.

Particular thanks to Larry Boadt, C.S.P., Michael Hunt, C.S.P., and Donald Brophy, my editors at Paulist Press.

---

*Under the title "Integrity: the Long Walk" in *Eureka Street* from December 1998 to July/August 1999. *Eureka Street* is a magazine of public affairs, the arts, and theology, published ten times a year by Jesuit Publications, P.O. Box 553, Richmond VIC 3121, Australia.

PREFACE

SINCE THE BEGINNING of the human race, a deeply rooted archaic religious conviction has been: Be good to the gods and they will be good to you. If we take care of God, God will take care of us. As a primal attitude, its influence varies; sometimes strong, sometimes not. It is usually elusive and subliminal, but usually there. Of course, it is only one element in the religious equation.

Much ink has been spilled and much passion spent on the importance of our loving God. Too little importance has been given to the passion that might be characteristic of God's loving us.

The acceptance of God's unconditional love for us has major consequences for the religious spirit. It challenges us to a level of commitment to the divine that is almost unheard of in religious literature. St. Teresa's "though you damn me, I will love you still" is the peak expression of human selfless love. What is the impact on us when we turn the phrase around: "Were I damnable, you would love me still"?

Unconditional love can be met only with utter love in return. Of course, such absolute love of God is certainly not the condition of most of us, so truth demands that memory will not allow us to forget the love that we have lacked.

For those who freely accept God's unconditional love, their acceptance has enormous consequences. They cannot pay God off, for they are loved by God. They cannot beg God in prayer, because they don't beg those who love them. They cannot look on others without realizing the mystery of God's unconditional love for them too. There is no escape from social justice and respect for human dignity and integrity. Even this world of ours, with all its defects, cannot be seen as a place of exile and evil, but as God's beloved creation, crying out to be improved and made just. Our lives cannot be imagined as a time of testing, for we are loved by God; our lives can only be a time of growing and maturing.

With a divine judge, the wicked are somehow punished and the rest of us are instinctively secure. With an unconditionally loving God, this world is evidently not open to our moral calculations; the good get cancer. Without the order assured by a God who judges, we are insecure, left with only our trust in God, trusting God to love us—and no more. A God who can be counted on to be there always; helpless to change things perhaps, but there, warmly and passionately and supportively, much like an utterly committed friend—and no more.

It is a vision of our world where God is not to be placated, because God is loving. It is a vision of the world where fear and anxiety before God yield to trust and love. Love that God has for us; love that we have for God. Our behavior flows from that. I do not want to spend eternity knowing that I am loved by God and being fully aware that my behavior has fallen shamefully short of what it might have been.

It is a vision of life where there is no currying favor with God, easing vague anxieties. No payment of dues in return for divine good will. No doing what God wants because it is God's will—but because we both want it. Just the integrity of who I am and my deepening acceptance that the ultimate accomplishment of my life is me. The ultimate mystery of our lives may be God's unconditional love for us. To live in this context is to rise above the oldest archaism of the human spirit. The invitation is to aspire to a level of spirit-filled existence that so far too few have managed to sustain for more than fleeting moments: a disclaimer of self-interest in divine order and a freedom to be loved and to love in the disorder of life's experience, to accept in faith God's unconditional love and faithfully to respond to it. It is a challenge; it is not easy.

OVERVIEW

IN FACING CHRISTIAN FAITH'S challenge to accept an unconditionally loving God, we can end up facing issues akin to those raised by some of Christianity's sharpest critics. For Albert Camus:

> Historic Christianity has only replied to this protest against evil by the Annunciation of the Kingdom and then of Eternal Life—accompanied by a demand for faith. But suffering exhausts hope and faith and then is left alone and unexplained. The toiling masses, worn out with suffering and death, are masses without God. Our place is henceforth at their side, far from teachers, old or new. Historic Christianity postpones, to a point beyond the span of history, the cure of evil and murder which are, nevertheless, experienced within the span of history. (*The Rebel*, 1951)

The compassion and service of practical Christianity dispute Camus. Both the insistence on the "kingdom" as a challenge for the present rather than a hope for the end of time and Vatican II's insistence on breadth of outreach emphasize a shift in the understanding that Camus is calling "historic Christianity." Any theoretical truth in the charge brought by Camus is challenged by the belief that God is with the toiling masses, being with us all as one who loves rather than presiding over us all as one who judges.

For Ignatius Loyola, founder of the Jesuits, within Christianity and within the span of history the challenge to the human spirit is to commit to the camp of Christ's poor—rather than siding with the powerful and proud—and so to see God in all and to seek God in all. The masses are not without God; God is to be found already with the masses, inviting us to join and take "our place…at their side." For Camus, "now is born that strange joy which helps one live and die, and which we shall never again renounce to a later time." For me—and surely, however expressed, for many who have taken their place at the side of those "worn out with suffering and death"—that "strange joy" is the absurdity of faith that we are loved by the God who is with us in all of our living, our toil, our suffering, and our dying. The cross, what Paul names as the absurdity of Christ crucified (1 Cor 1:23–24), is the symbol of God's commitment to the rebel against all that is oppression and injustice—anywhere!

CLASSICAL CHRISTIANITY is challenged by the prospect of faith in a deeply and unconditionally loving God. Originally, I believed the acceptance of a loving God involved a significant but relatively minor shift of attitude. After all, it was on so many people's lips. The more I worked with it, the more I realized that the acceptance in faith of God's unconditional love was not only hugely significant; it entailed major changes of attitude. Finally, it has come home to me that the major changes of attitude required by a commitment in faith to God's unconditional love for us add up to a significant revision of the face of Christian faith.

It is a revision that touches our theological attitude to human life in its beginning, its middle, and its end. Its beginning: for a deeply loving God we can hardly be second best; a classical understanding of original sin is in trouble. Its end: a deeply loving God is in love with us as we are, not waiting for what we might become; classical understandings of the kingdom are in trouble. Its middle: if we are what God wants and loves, the understanding of Jesus Christ's incarnation, death, and resurrection as redemptive and salvific needs a rethink. That is a lot.

For the middle of life there are further implications, involving a rethinking of attitudes about our life, our world, and our destiny. With a deeply loving God, our life is hardly a time of testing but a time of growing and maturing. With a deeply loving God, our world is hardly a valley of tears in which we, poor banished children of Eve, mourn and weep, to borrow the words of that familiar prayer, Hail, Holy Queen; instead, it is God's beloved creation, crying out to be improved and made just. With a deeply loving God, our destiny hardly lies in the choice of heaven and hell, but perhaps in an eternity of knowing that we are loved and of holding on to our memories in their entirety.

If we go a step further, there are implications for our prayers and our expectations. We seldom plead with those who love us. Should we in prayer plead with the God we believe loves us deeply? Acceptance of a loving God and observation of our world combine to suggest limits on aspects of the exercise of God's power. Are there limits to what we may expect of God and therefore what we might ask of God?

The most major shift may be in the images we have of God and of ourselves. How radically is our image of God reshaped if we take seriously belief in God as deeply, passionately, and unconditionally loving us? How radically must we rework our own self-image if we accept ourselves as lovable—as deeply, passionately, and unconditionally loved by God?

The energy for this vision comes out of traditional and orthodox Christian faith. I am a Roman Catholic, and I write out of the faith that is mine; across believing communities, the shifts needed will vary. I believe the claims made are grounded firmly in the basics of Christian faith. The conviction that underlies this vision is simple and it is sound classical theology: Anything we can do, God can do better, especially when it comes to loving and forgiving.

The vision sketched here is a belief that is chosen. It is a matter of bringing elements of faith together in brighter light and sharper focus. It does not make and cannot make a total or exclusive claim on Christian faith. It is a belief available to be chosen within Christian faith; it is one position among others. Such chosen belief is commitment to a point of view, while recognizing that it might be wrong (with acknowledgments to John Polkinghorne and ultimately Michael Polanyi, *Personal Knowledge*, 1958).

The options open to Christian faith and living are many, but I believe they range around two poles:

1. A commitment to moral behavior and full human living, because it is right and because it is God's will for us, which we accept and respect, and in which we come to fullness of life with God.

2. A commitment to moral behavior and full human living, because it is right and because of God's deep love for us, which we accept and return, and in which we come to fullness of life with God.

The difference in words here is slight; the difference in life can be very great. From another angle, does our basic attitude emphasize appropriate behavior as a *condition* for being loved by God or as a *consequence* of being loved by God?

What seemed at first to be no big deal turns out to have far-reaching implications. And then, in reflecting on our relationship with God, we must always leave room for mystery. God is not God who does not escape us into mystery.

Faith's challenge goes wider than just to Christian faith. It challenges believers, and we are all of us believers.* Atheists believe in a world without God. Theists believe in a world with God. Agnostics believe they cannot know

---

*Joseph Ratzinger quotes a story from Martin Buber to make this point (J. Ratzinger, *Introduction to Christianity*, 1969, pp. 20–21). He writes: "Both the believer and the unbeliever...share doubt *and* belief, if they do not hide away from themselves and from the truth of their being." In my language, that makes both believer and unbeliever believers.

enough to commit themselves. And faith's challenge is not just that—it is also invitation.

Faith in a loving God challenges belief in a world without God. Does atheism offer more meaning? Faith in a loving God challenges belief in a world with God. Do we theists really accept a loving God? Faith in a loving God challenges agnosticism. Does lack of certainty justify lack of commitment. How much certainty do we demand in our lives before we commit ourselves? How long must we be invited?

Faith's challenge is wide. Do I accept God's love—for me? for others? for the wicked? for the world? for ever? The invitation is there.

Talk is easy. Have we committed ourselves to accepting what we talk about? Many people now talk about a loving God. It is one of the changes to the face of faith in recent times. Listening to what such people say and write, I am not sure that most really accept the loving God they talk about. It is time for the challenge to be faced, for the invitation to be accepted.

1 INTRODUCTION

*A God abounding in steadfast love
and faithfulness.*
Exodus 34:6

I AM UTTERLY CONVINCED that the best under-standing of Judeo-Christian faith has to be centered on God's unconditional love for us.

Plenty of people today talk about a loving God. I am not sure people are taking on board the full reality of the loving God they're talking about. It's in the Bible. It's in the language of modern spirituality. But discovering that we are passionately loved by God is a long way from being the central experience of many Christians. The words are there, but sometimes the reality isn't.

There are plenty of reasons why it shouldn't be. Fear can be more effective than love in getting us moving, at least in the short term. Sheer goodness or the prospect of reward can move us to action, but it has often been judged more immediately effective to wield a big stick.

When I was young, we were taught about the difference between a sorrow that was motivated by the fear of hell and a sorrow that was motivated by pure love for God. Alas, the "pure love" was our love for God. We were never invited to take seriously the reality of God's love for us. Not then; not now.

Over my years as a Roman Catholic, a Jesuit, a student of theology, and a lover of the Older Testament, this has been uncomfortable, an irritant. More and more, our theology seemed to be selling God short. We talked about a loving God, but so much of what we said and did and prayed reflected other images of God, other ideas about God. I want an integrity in my faith where, if I accept a loving God, I am not at the same time holding on to a whole bunch of things that do not fit with a God who loves. So now I am simply putting on paper the struggle in myself for what I would call the integrity of my faith.

From Christian beginnings in the Newer Testament we have the claim: "In this is love, not that we loved God but that he loved us.…We love [God] because he first loved us" (1 Jn 4:10,19). There is a traditional hymn that says: "I love thee, O thou Lord most high, because thou first hast loved me."* I want to explore the possible shape of a vision of Christian faith that takes this love of God for us seriously.

John doesn't mince words about the place of love in our faith: "There is no fear in love, but perfect love casts

*It is from Rev. Edward Caswall, C.O. (1814–78), inspired by the "Take, Lord, and receive" of St. Ignatius Loyola. "Because thou first hast loved me" is not explicit in Ignatius's prayer, but flows from its context.

out fear; for fear has to do with punishment, and whoever fears has not reached perfection in love" (1 Jn
4:18). But even here this is about our love for God.
What about emphasis on God's love for us? If we take
God's love for us seriously and accept it, that ought to be
the end of fear. But as I listen and look around me, it's
not. Fear of punishment and a few other things are still
there—often an odd anxiety that shows up as confidence
that God will take care of us, *because we've paid our dues.*
Unlovely and unloving; we fear God won't love us freely.
So there's a struggle for integrity.

I AM NOT SURE what triggered this struggle in me.
It probably goes back to my earliest years, but since I
don't have access to it there, I have to start later. I
have a vivid memory of listening to a talk in the late
1970s. I was part of a group doing a workshop with an
Indian Jesuit, Father Tony de Mello, widely known for
his work in spirituality.* Tony was sitting on the edge of
a table, talking to the group, one leg swinging rhythmi-
cally as he spoke.

"You know, I pay Almighty God the compliment of
believing that God is at least a little better than I am."

At the back of the group, I felt a surge of indignation.
Why did this learned man who spoke so eloquently of
prayer and of God and who could make such eminently
sound theological sense, why did this man make such

---

*It has been reported that de Mello's writings were criticized by
the Vatican's Congregation for the Doctrine of the Faith in August
1998; he was accused of "an exaggerated apophaticism." I doubt
that this criticism touches what is used here.

stupid egotistic remarks that could undermine his whole credibility? He continued:

> You know, sometimes I hear people talking about God and I think to myself, if people preached about me half the things they preach about God, I would hide under the bed in shame. I mean, you hear people talk about earning God's love and what they would need to do to win God's forgiveness. Nobody earns my love; it is gift. Nobody wins my forgiveness; I give it to them. Is God really so different?

The fire of my indignation was doused. "Earning God's love" was a phrase I had heard often enough and it needed only a glimmer of light to reveal how inadequate it was. We do not earn love. It is a gift that is given us. I'd had more than enough experience watching people try to earn others' love to know how painfully destructive it was. Why, then, all the talk in liturgy and spirituality of being made worthy of God's love, of becoming acceptable in God's sight, and so on? What sense did that make if God already loved us?

I remember another experience about ten years later. I had given a couple of talks to a group of theological students in the lead-up to Easter, basically on the place of a loving God in the celebration of Easter. One of the students approached me afterward in the parking lot.

"I was fascinated by your talks," she said. "Can I ask you just one question?"

"Sure. Go ahead."

"Well, I'm not certain that I got you right, but were you talking about God as one who loves, as a lover and not as a judge? I have always been brought up to think of God as a judge."

I was taken aback. "I've never really thought of it in those terms. But yes, if you put it that way, I definitely want to say that God is a lover rather than a judge. Once you use those two terms, surely the primacy has to be given to God as one who loves."

"That opens up a whole new range of thought for me," she said. "I'll have to reflect on it for a while."

"Happy Easter!" I said, and we each drove off. I drove home pondering the idea of God as one who loves or God as one who judges. Surely the primacy had to be given to God as one who loves. I chewed it over for a very long time; I still do. At one level, it is easy to grasp; at another level, it goes very deep. The two terms polarize much religious experience and religious language for me. One or the other lies behind a lot of the language and ritual we use in relation to God. Humanly speaking, judging and loving are polar opposites. What about with God?

At some point, I read James Joyce's *Portrait of the Artist as a Young Man*. In the context of a final school retreat, Joyce has his hero, Stephen Dedalus, use similarly polarized language: at the instant of death, "God, who had long been merciful, would then be just." Together in the retreat-giver's images are God the lover ("He loved you as only a God can love") and God the judge ("God would not be God if He did not punish the transgressor"). I thought to myself: "God, who had long been merciful, would then be just"—that's too easy and it's not fair to God. In human language, so sudden a switch to the judge inevitably means that we are not taking the lover seriously.

Certainly, we sometimes don't take God's love seriously enough. At a recent liturgical celebration, the auditorium was huge and packed with people. The entry procession took forever to squeeze its way through the crowd, but finally it got to the altar and the presider turned to address the congregation. First, a big sign of the cross and a few words of introduction. Then, to get the liturgy under way, the priest called us to prayer with the words, "Let us beg for God's mercy." It was worse than the Roman Missal's bald "Let us call to mind our sins." Perhaps what followed was not in his script and the long procession to the altar had got him flustered. Anyway, he added, "Let us beg for God's love." To my ear, that was worse, much worse. The eucharist is about God's love for us, Christ's life given in love for us. And here we were being invited not just to pray for what God had already given us, but to beg for it: "Let us beg for God's love." I was jarred and upset by the distance between language and faith. I've heard of begging for mercy, but begging for love? Never! And anyway, we have it; we are loved. God loves us; that is at the core of our faith.

THERE IS A LACK OF INTEGRITY in a formulation of faith that proclaims a loving God and then talks or behaves in ways that deny a loving God. All language about God reaches into mystery, but does it have to abandon integrity? That is my struggle. That is what these pages are about.

These are personal musings, my musings. I am a New Zealander, one of those people born between Vatican I and Vatican II; I have been a Jesuit in Australia for almost half a century. I've had as good a basic theological education as France could offer in the mid-1960s followed by scriptural studies in Rome and the United States, and I've been privileged to spend my life since learning from the word of God in the Older Testament, and learning from other experience too. These are personal musings, as honest as I can make them. They have been valuable to me in my faith, my prayer, and my work. If they strike a chord, well and good. If not, leave them thoughtfully to one side.

With the encyclical *Divino Afflante Spiritu* in 1943, the Roman Catholic Church opened its way to a new vision of the possibilities for understanding the word of God in scripture. Today, we have a new vision too of our world and our universe that was unthinkable a few decades ago, with developments in so many areas from communications and travel to computers and mass media, and above all in physics, politics, and psychology. Our world is radically different from the world of our grandparents, radically different! Now is an appropriate time to look afresh at the vision of our faith and to reemphasize as the central Christian experience the mystery that we are passionately loved by God.

Note that this chapter opened with a quote from Exodus 34: "A God abounding in steadfast love and faithfulness." It would be dishonest not to signal what comes next in verse 7: "forgiving iniquity and transgression and sin, yet by no means clearing the guilty, but visiting the iniquity of the parents upon the children..."—as if those whose iniquity was forgiven weren't guilty. This is not a rider or a corrective; it is a contradiction. On the one hand, God forgives iniquity; on the other, "by no means." Exodus 34:6–7 brings together an unusually large number of the phrases traditionally used in the description of God, therefore expressing several perspectives—reflecting on the nature of God and also perhaps adverting to the nature of sin, with its sometimes unavoidable consequences and its possible impact on several generations (see Ex 20:5-6; Nm 14:18; Dt 5:9-10; Is 43:25; Jer 32:18; Jl 2:13; Jon 4:2; Na 1:3; Pss 86:15, 103:8, 145:8; Neh 9:17). The Bible often retains contrasting perspectives; for example, there is no single view of creation, flood, exodus, wilderness, conquest, monarchy, or even providence. Israel offered choices to its theologians and its storytellers. The Bible does not impose thought on us but invites us to think.

A Cautionary Tale

Howlers happen, but whoppers should not happen in Bible translations. That one got away leads to the question: What sort of widespread automatic mindset let it pass? Why was no one alarmed enough to check? How did it get past so many smart, observant editorial eyes?

In a key passage of the book of Deuteronomy, the *Jerusalem Bible* translates as follows:

> You have this day made this declaration about Yahweh: that he will be your God, but only if you follow his ways, keep his statutes, his commandments, his ordinances, and listen to his voice. (Dt 26:17)

What is horribly wrong here is that one little word in Hebrew has been turned into a formal condition by three words in English: "but only if" (original French: "mais à la condition que"). The one little word in Hebrew is *wĕ* regularly translated as "and," "also," "or," "but," "if," "so," "then," or "when," "since," "seeing," "though," and so on. The precise meaning depends on the context and is usually clear in the context. Nowhere in the Older Testament is it rendered by so definite a condition as "but only if." The same mistake is repeated in the next verse. The translation imposes an interpretation on the verse that the Hebrew does not demand and may indeed deny. In the NRSV, for example, this verse reads:

> Today you have obtained the LORD'S agreement: to
> be your God; and for you to walk in his ways, to
> keep his statutes, his commandments, and his ordi-
> nances, and to obey him.

Guilty of this howler was one of the great French
exegetes of our time. What made him do it? At the least, it
is likely to have been the conviction that God could not
love us unless we keep the law, in the Older Testament at
any rate. What an awful theology. God can be our God, but
only if we keep the law. What Deuteronomy has is that
God is our God AND we will keep the law.

There's a world of difference. The person who says "If
you do what I demand, I will love you" is in deep trouble from the point of view of relationship. It is quite different to say, "I love you, and I'd be grateful if you do
what I ask." The first is a *condition* placed prior to love;
the second is a *consequence* of love.

Earlier in the book, Deuteronomy said it plainly and
clearly: "For you are a people consecrated to Yahweh
your God; it is you that Yahweh your God has chosen to
be his very own people...." (Dt 7:6). No "ifs" or "buts"
about that. The learned translator got it right that time.
Deuteronomy got it right both times. Do we dare get it
right at those times when it matters?

If we believe that our keeping God's law is a condition
of our being loved by God, then we are believing that at
least in part God's love is earned. When will we accept
that God's love for us is gratuitous, is gift, is grace?

There is a prayer in the Roman Missal that reads: "God
our Father, you have promised to remain for ever with
those who do what is just and right" (Sixth Sunday in

Ordinary Time). Loving God, what about the rest of us? If we were to add a little rider like that to the marriage vows—for richer, for poorer, in good times and in bad, in sickness and in health, to love and to cherish for as long as we do what is just and right—divorce rates would go through the roof.

2 THE PRELIMINARIES

I will sing of your steadfast love, O LORD, forever.
Psalm 89:1

IT WOULD BE GOOD TO GET STRAIGHT TO the vision of faith offered by belief in a loving God. We can't paint that picture unless we are well aware of what we are doing and the limits involved. We need to look at three things and a fourth: the worth of our talk about God, the issue of our priorities, our appeal to ordinary experience, and fourth, our fear of God (which will need a chapter all to itself).

Few things are certain in theology, but one is sure. If we finally believe that at last we have got everything right about God, we can be sure that we're wrong. "God" is a name we give to a relational being, but more than that. "God" is also a name we use in faith to give expression to a wide and diverse range of experience. What faith names "God" is a mystery that defies any attempt to get everything about it right. It helps to remember this when reflecting on our God-talk, our priorities, our experience, and even our fear of God.

GOD-TALK. There are all sorts of ways of talking about God and all sorts of people who like to talk about God in different ways. I do not want to exclude anything that is valuable in faith to someone else. On the other hand, I do want to contemplate the possibility that we may have to make a choice about what is primary in the language we use about God. There are various languages we can use to talk about God, various metaphors we can apply to God. If they conflict with each other—and if our human speech and thought is not to be too destructively incoherent—one of them may require priority over the others.

Lover, judge, and patron or benefactor are all metaphors that are used of God. Lover and judge are easy enough to understand. In human reality, they are opposed. One who loves is by definition biased; that's what it means to be in love. One who judges is by definition supposed to be unbiased; that's what it means to be a judge. James Joyce's retreat-giver (in *Portrait of the Artist as a Young Man*) presented God as both loving and judging. One of these has to have priority over the other. In Joyce's text, God as loving is primary while we are alive; God as judging takes over the instant we are dead. I don't find that this solution respects God's love. It has an inconsistency in it that denies the love. For me, God's love has to have priority over God's justice. There is a place for God's justice, but God's love is primary. We have to take it seriously.

A patron is almost an outmoded term, restricted to royalty and sporting clubs. The reality, however, is still around. Religious behavior has a lot to do with God as patron-cum-benefactor. In this sense, a patron is a protector and a figure who can provide influential support and assistance. Today's political lobbyists do not talk about their patrons, but they are interested in people who can wield influence on behalf of their causes. As I understand church history, patron saints were patterned on the patrons at court who exercised influence on emperors and kings. When we expect God to respond to our intercessions, to protect us, and to exercise beneficial influence in our lives, we may be treating God as a patron-cum-benefactor. And that's different from both a lover and a judge.

Using human language to talk about God has its problems—but we've nothing else. It is hard enough to get words and images to work for us in human situations, describing human experience; they let us down, though, when we turn to God. The classic rules for the process of language about God are simple, but not all that helpful. First, whatever we experience as positive and good is affirmed of God, as belonging to God. Second, whatever is negative and not good is denied of God. Third, whatever is taken from human experience as positive and good, and so affirmed of God, has to be elevated, or exalted, to mirror the radical difference between ourselves and God. It is this third element that makes words and images fail. It is all three elements taken together that makes the process possible.

PRIORITIES ARE IMPORTANT. My struggle is for integrity and coherence in our talk about God. The language we use about God is a matter of choice; a choice we have either made for ourselves or inherited from others. For coherence, each of us may need to assess the priority we give to particular metaphors. For me, the primary metaphor is of God as loving. If judge and patron-cum-benefactor—and others—are to have their place, for me they must be subordinate to faith in God as loving. On the surface, it sounds acceptable; if we go deep with it, faith in God as loving does not come easily.

We will need to talk about mystery, but not yet. At this point, it is important that, in all the fragility and vulnerability and inadequacy of human language, we recognize faith's invitation to allow one image and one language to have priority for us. I believe we have to grow into and gently choose a primary metaphor. To allow the metaphors of judge and lover, for example, to subvert each other is to risk a destructive ambivalence in our relationship with God.

If we are to speak of God as loving, we have to be aware of aspects of the language of judging or of aspects of behavior toward patrons or benefactors that are incompatible with the language and behavior of one who loves. We may need all the metaphors to talk about God, but I do not believe it is healthy for us to have them on the same footing. Maybe sometimes we play them off against each other as a cover-up. Is there perhaps a fear in us that we need to cover up, a fear of accepting that we are loved by God?

EXPERIENCE IS IMPORTANT. I have been talking about human experience—because that is all we have. I don't have any direct experience of God. I cannot speak for the experience of others. But none of us can touch and see and hear God as we touch and see and hear others. As the small boy said when urged not to be afraid of being alone in the dark, because God was there: "But God doesn't have any skin on!" In the exploration of our human experience God is disclosed to us. I read the Bible and experience myself attracted to an image of God or repelled by an image of God. I have to explore the totality of my experience to discover God and to discover what God is for me. Our experiences and discoveries will be different for each of us. "Gifts differing": we are so very different and we should be grateful for it.

Should I turn to the church for a clear understanding of God? Confusion is there too. God is spoken of as a loving Father whom we beg for mercy. That is confusing, because I never asked my own father for mercy. Our loving God is described as "God of power and might" and we petition God as we might a patron or a benefactor. In the Christian community, we may even ask saints to plead with God for us. I am confused, because I have never pleaded with someone who loved me. If they love me, they do what they can for me without any pleading from me. I may need to ask, to let my needs be known. But pleading? No!

For a long time now, I've put language about God to a simple test. Does it square with a similar situation in human experience? I use this test particularly for language of love and forgiveness. We express our need to be loved, our gratitude for being loved, our sorrow for the hurts we inflict, but we do not beg. Humanly, we don't beg those who love us for their love or their forgiveness.

Should we of God? If we do, are we failing to accept the reality of God's love for us?

The touchstone of human experience is all very well, but we are not God. We say that God is "utterly other," radically different from us. We may not like it, but we do know that we are not God. So perhaps what is not appropriate in human experience is appropriate to God. I have no problem with that. All I ask is that we run our God-talk by the test of human experience—and then think about it.

It is important to be clear on what is meant here about words and God. I am not so concerned whether our words adequately reflect something of the reality of God. I am more concerned with the fact that our words about God express how we relate to God. What I am claiming, then, for some of us, is that our words and the human attitudes they reflect may need to have a certain coherence; they may need to reflect something of the reality that is us. The union of opposites in the mystery of God is all right for some; for others, it does not attend to the disjointedness within ourselves. The union of opposites in the mystery of God is one thing; I'm afraid that, for me, the union of opposites in my experience of myself and my language is another. This is not a study of the validity of human language about God. It is a reflection on our attitudes toward God and the validity of the language we use to express them.

In human experience, love is a gift; we don't earn it. God's love too is a gift; we don't earn it. Being loved is not essentially a matter of being worthy. That love is gift is not pious jargon. People may find us lovable, but that does not mean they love us. Perhaps one of them chooses to love us; that love is gift. The others do not give it; one does. Loving and being loved is a highly complex experience. To those who love us, we are lovable. But we don't earn their love. They give it to us. What about God? In God's eyes, are we lovable? Does it make sense to talk about earning God's love and being made worthy of God's love? God's love is gift, given us.

Forgiveness is fascinating and just as complex a gift as love. Job screams at God, "If I sin…why do you not pardon my transgression and take away my iniquity?" (Jb 7:20–21) Isaiah gives us this self-description from God: "I, I am the One who blots out your transgressions for my own sake, and I will not remember your sins" (Is 43:25). Forgiveness is given by the lover, ultimately for the lover's own sake. Forgiveness is not merely a charity I extend to the offender; it is also and above all a gift I offer to myself for my own healing and my wholeness.

Can we earn forgiveness? Is there any point in begging for forgiveness? What is our own experience? Where love is strong, forgiveness can be there for us before there is any movement on our part. Something special happens when forgiveness is given fulfillment by its recognition and acceptance. Sorrow and understanding can be involved in healing. The words needed may be "I'm sorry," and it may take time before it is clear that the words are real. But forgiveness is given, not earned. Healing may take time; the forgiveness is gift. Where there is love, the gift will not be withheld. Is that where we are with God?

We have to work with analogy and metaphor. We have nothing else for language about God. We have to run our language about God through the test of human experience. Thinking about it may convince us that things are different with God. But we have to think about it. We may have to realize that things are not so different, that our attitude is inappropriate and something has to change. And we will probably spend our lives struggling with the issue of what is primary for us in our belief about God and how God relates to us.

Are we lobbying God for our favorite causes and, above all, for our well-being? Do we relate to God as our judge, favorable to us when we're good and turned from us when we're not? Do we believe in God as genuinely in love with us, rejoicing in our welfare and pained by our failures? Is our primary experience the overwhelming mystery that God loves us unconditionally?

The Score: Wisdom 0—Mystery 1

In biblical times, there was a story about a legendary figure called Job who had a reputation for being unbelievably good. According to the story, God made the mistake of pointing him out to the public prosecutor (Hebrew: the satan).

> "Good, isn't he?" said God.
> "Does all right because of it, doesn't he?" said the prosecutor.

God—most improperly, we must admit—allowed the satan to strip Job of all he had, his children included, and then to inflict an appalling disease on Job himself. Much to the satan's disappointment, Job came through the ordeal with flying colors. He did not curse God. After the first affliction, he said, "Blessed be the name of the LORD" (Jb 1:21). After the second, he said: "Shall we receive the good at the hand of God, and not receive the bad?" (Jb 2:10)

With this issue settled and with this little parable told to show that people do not necessarily love God simply in the hope of doing well because of it, the Book of Job moves on to a much weightier issue. Basically, is the great wisdom tradition of the Older Testament right when it sees suffering as merited by human sin, sees it functioning for human purification, and sees the appropriate response to suffering to be pious prayer that will be rewarded? Job's friends endorse this. Job says it is outrageous rubbish. At the end, when the chips are down, God sides with Job; the friends are wrong. We are left with a puzzle: humans are not responsible; God is not hostile; suffering happens. Even in stories, such puzzles are called mystery. Love hardly rates a mention in the book of Job. Perhaps we need to hold together human suffering and God's love.

> There is suffering in human life and we do not know why it should be. Some we can see as the result of the gift of human freedom. Some we can see as the result of the forces of nature. Some is utterly inscrutable, with an apparent cruelty of fate for which there is no explanation. Some suffering can be ennobling, but not all. Some lives that are burdened with heavy suffering can be rich and fulfilling lives, but why should it have to be so? Railing against God does nothing to help, unless it ventilates an anger that were better directed against the arbitrariness of misfortune. Job's diatribes against God show there is no solution to be sought in that direction.
>
> Instead there is the encounter with mystery. The mystery of human life which in its vulnerability and frailty can be infinitely precious and treasured. The mystery of human love which can surmount extraordinary pain and suffering. The mystery of divine love which must suffer and grieve with us in our hurt and misery, but which—as we can say to each other—says also to us: "you are precious in my eyes, and honored, and I love you." (Campbell, *Study Companion*, 1989/1992)

There is no human language that can cope with the passion of God's love and the experience of human suffering. Yet there is scarcely any other area of human life where it is so essential that we do not remain silent.

The incarnation and the cross of Jesus say it best.

3 THE FEAR

There is no fear in love, but perfect love casts out fear; for fear has to do with punishment, and whoever fears has not reached perfection in love.
1 John 4:18

OR MANY, FEAR AND LOVE DO NOT GO together. Often, fear is allied with confusion and the combination inhibits the acceptance of love. The reality is there; we need to look at it. Left unexamined, fear can corrosively undermine acceptance of God's love.

I don't love those I fear. So where does that leave me with God? It is natural to be afraid of overwhelming force: an earthquake, a landslide, a tornado, a raging sea, someone who is a lot bigger and meaner than I am. The idea of a creator is associated with overwhelming power; God is often spoken of as almighty and all-powerful. If I feel it is out of the question to refuse a demand, it is natural to fear what may be asked. Most people feel that way about God. According to many psychologists, intimacy is what almost everyone wants and what almost everyone fears just about as badly. Understandably: intimacy needs vulnerability. Accepting a loving God inevitably leads to our intimacy with God. Three strikes against the love of God—all of them spelled f-e-a-r! A powerful God, a demanding God, and a loving God; all giving us cause to fear God.

Some people do love and also fear. Such love and fear would, I believe, involve complex factors: past and present processes, rational and nonrational elements, adult and child aspects, the impact of doubt, and so on. I do not know. It may be more realistic to say that fear holds us back from loving unreservedly. Fear puts restraints on love. Trust matters. How do we come to trust God?

A POWERFUL GOD. If we believe God to be creator of our universe, we can hardly dissociate God from overwhelming power. Not that we are tossed around by it as we might be by an earthquake, a tornado, or a raging sea. But we're confronted by it whenever we open our eyes or whenever we stop to think.

No matter what we know about our universe, if we accept belief in a creator God we are claiming God as a being of immense outreach and power. Our solar system, with its one star, is big enough: the sun, our moon, and the planets. A galaxy is vastly bigger; for example, our own galaxy, the Milky Way. Astronomers say there may be as many as a thousand million stars in the bigger galaxies. I can be wide-eyed with wonder at the experience of thousands upon thousands of individuals all crowded into a single sports arena, but nothing like a million. The reality of some ten million people below as I fly over Los Angeles is staggering. I have not flown over China. Astronomers go further and calculate there are more than a hundred thousand million galaxies out there, receding into the distance at incredible speeds. Believers in God hold that all this vast universe rests—metaphorically—in the palm of God's hand. Belief in God is stretched, but belief in nothing may be stretching it even more.

Have too many of us today lost the knack for wonder? The ancients knew wonder well enough:

> When I look at your heavens, the work of your fingers,
>   the moon and the stars that you have established;
> what are human beings that you are mindful of them
>   mortals that you care for them? (Ps 8:3–4)

I can get around the wonder intellectually by letting God be God and settling for the limits of my own human mind. I can't get away from the fear quite so easily—a very human fear, but mine. What do I do with it? I can ignore my fear. If I do, it doesn't go away and it does impact on my relationship with God. Very simply: I don't love those I fear. If fear is there, it is going to affect any love in my relationship with God. John said, "There is no fear in love, but perfect love casts out fear" (1 Jn 4:18). But my love of God is far from perfect and my acceptance of God's love needs help.

I don't see any way of banishing this elemental fear. It is my natural reaction as creature in the presence of my Creator. I have to look at it, face it, own it. I think I have to put it in its place. That's where priorities are important. I don't want fear to have a high priority in my faith. Perhaps the place for my fear is alongside faith in the incarnation. This awesome, all-powerful creator God freely chose to become a human being, figured beginning as an utterly helpless infant in a feedtrough and ending as a victim on a cross. Sheer wonder can give fear a run for its money. Can we fear a God who loves enough for that?

A DEMANDING GOD. Are we free to say no to God? If we aren't, are we forced back into fear, a fear of the demand that cannot be refused? A relationship is humanly suspect if the freedom to say no isn't there. What happens in our relationship to God? Is that so different?

It is not fashionable among Christian believers to think of saying no to God; but it has to be thought about. The "rich young man" said no to Jesus. Everybody I have talked with believes that Jesus still loved him as he walked away (Mk 10:21–22). Finding plausible examples of our being free to say no to God goes against the grain, but I think they are there. The question is not the theological issue of whether God has a particular will for us. The question rises for those who believe God has a preference in certain cases.

Someone has a choice between two jobs, one secure and solid with the certainty of a financial future and the other risky and uncertain with the challenging possibility of changing a bit of the world. One of these jobs may be felt to carry with it a strong call from God. There has to be the possibility of saying no, and, as we walk away, of knowing ourselves loved by God. Objectivity and moral wisdom are not the issue.

Conscience is. The conscientious belief is that God wants one of the options. Such options may be found in the choices of career, of partner, of schooling for children, of medical procedures, and so on.

A LOVING GOD. Accepting the love of God is not impossible; it just isn't easy. Where God's vastness is concerned, if I am certain of God's unconditional love for me, I am not afraid. Those who love me unconditionally will not harm me, so no cause for fear. First, though, I have to accept that unconditional love. When I am unconditionally loved, I ought to be able to say no. Most of us don't feel that way about God. Maybe I should, but first I have to accept God's unconditional love. Deep down, it is scary to accept love, to accept my being utterly loved—scary, but quite different from fear of another.

It sounds odd to call love scary. At first blush, it can seem ridiculous; on reflection, it can be seen as right. I'm not sure why love is scary. Is it the fear of having my shallowness revealed? Of being found uninteresting or boring? Of being vulnerable to rejection? Of being hurt? Of dependence? Of loss? Has it something to do with losing myself to the other? What if my beloved might want what I'm unwilling to give? Ultimately, is lack of trust the basic block to intimacy?

The love of God is scary. To accept my love for God is scary; to accept God's love for me, even more so.

F EAR OF GOD GETS IN THE WAY OF accepting God's love. Perhaps not at a surface level, but certainly at that deep visceral level where it matters.

Until I face my fear of God, the reality of our human fear of God, I can't accept God's unconditional love. It is all very well for me to adopt a pious tone of voice and speak of "reverential awe before the majesty of infinite power"; what matters is its effect on my relationship with God. My fear may be eased by belief in God's justice or God's love. But the fear is there.

Respect and reverential awe are there too. They are close to fear; they are not the same as fear. They too can get in the way of our accepting God's deep, passionate, and unconditional love for us. Humanly speaking, we are not used to associating deep and passionate love with profound respect and reverential awe. We reverence and respect those we love, but that is different. Where God is concerned, our respect and reverence can get in the way of our accepting God's love. Fear gets in the way even more.

God's love for us is a central element of Christian faith and always has been. I believe that is true of Jewish faith too, but I don't know enough to make statements about others' faith. Our faith can be like a pudding. Central elements get mixed into a pudding with many other ingredients. It would be nice if faith was clear and straightforward; but it's not. God's love for us is a central ingredient in the mixture that is our faith; respect and reverence and fear are among the ingredients too, along with many others. The taste of a pudding depends on all the ingredients and the proportions they've been mixed in and the way they've been cooked. Where faith is concerned, we each make our own pudding. It is enough to recognize that fear of God is one of the ingredients of faith and is a force that can push belief in God's love for us into the background. In my experience, fearing God remains a very human activity, and not always a healthy one. It can be healthy, but not always. For me, fear has to move into the far background.

Scripture and liturgy don't necessarily help much to banish fear. "The fear of the LORD is the beginning of knowledge" (Prv 1:7).* "Fear of the LORD" gets an extensive press in the Older Testament. Even when contexts suggest a meaning closer to "the love of God," the overtones of fear remain. Passages in the gospels can intensify our fear. Remember Peter's "Go away from me, Lord, for I am a sinful man" (Lk 5:8) or the centurion's "Lord, do not trouble yourself, for I am not worthy to have you come under my roof" (Lk 7:6). Peter again: "You will never wash my feet" (Jn 13:8). We might talk about humility, but passages like these can confirm an unhealthy fear by injecting a false sense of unworthiness.

It is all very well for the gospel to say "Do not fear those who kill the body but cannot kill the soul"; that's the stuff of martyrs. When it goes on, "rather fear him who can destroy both soul and body in hell" (Mt 10:28), then it sounds as if it is positively encouraging fear of God. It is even stronger in Luke's gospel: "But I will

---

*LORD in small capitals here and elsewhere is used, following the RSV and NRSV tradition, to represent YHWH, the Hebrew personal name of Israel's God. As a rule, this name is not pronounced by Jews; it is not used in the Newer Testament, written in Greek. It is important that Christians avoid driving an unnecessary wedge between the Older and Newer Testaments.

warn you whom to fear: fear him who, after he has killed, has authority to cast into hell. Yes, I tell you, fear him!" (Lk 12:5) Other quotations, of course, point in other directions, but such passages reenforce a fear of God that is instinctive in human nature. Fear plays a larger role in faith than many of us might like to admit.

Our Roman Catholic liturgical language often emphasizes the "God of power and might." Immense power evokes fear. It can be a healthy fear, which is properly awe and respect, or it can be a destructive fear, which is afraid of being overwhelmed by superior power. I wonder what "power and might" evokes for us in our prayer. I know some for whom it is a source of terror.

Since I've become sensitive to the havoc that fear plays with faith, I often cringe over the emphasis on unrelieved divine power in liturgical language. What if our liturgy gave us a little more balance; for example, "almighty and ever-loving God" in place of "almighty and everlasting God," or at the Sanctus (Holy, holy, holy Lord) "God of life and love" instead of "God of power and might." Wouldn't it be challenging and just as true? Fear of God is all very well in its place, but it can be powerful and out of place and block our acceptance of God's love for us.

If I need to face my fear before I can accept God's love, the incarnation of Jesus Christ becomes very important for me, emotionally more than doctrinally. Jesus is the human face of God. Jesus sweated, and smiled, and wept. Jesus can take my hand in his, can take me in his embrace (see Mk 9:36; 10:16: he took them in his arms). Jesus, the Word made flesh, can bridge that fearful gap between creature and Creator. The incarnation helps me have a feel for the intimacy with God imaged in our walking with God in the evening (Gn 3:8) and that is open to us because we are precious in God's sight, and honored, and loved (Is 43:4). This is the intimacy that God's unconditional love offers us. To accept it, I have to face my fears and entrust myself to God's love. It is not easy!

Eavesdropping on Prayer

The funny thing is, of course, that an unconditionally loving God will only ask of us what is for our own good. But then, many of us are afraid of what might be best for us. Stupid, but true!

Imagine prayer that took the following shape:

> "My God, I'd feel a lot more comfortable talking to you if I wasn't afraid of what you may ask of me. There is a lot I don't want to give up."
>
> "My dear, try to realize that I love you very deeply and all I want for you is your own deepest happiness."
>
> "That's all very well, but surely that is going to involve my giving up something or changing something. I'm not sure I want to. I'm not sure I'm strong enough to."
>
> "Are you not sure that you want your own deepest happiness?"
>
> "Oh God, Job was right. You are a hard one to argue with."

Maybe we do have to change. Who knows? But if we are to change, we will be changing for our own good, for the sake of our own happiness. We would not change because God wants us to be good. We would change because we ourselves want what contributes to our own deepest happiness. Morality is aimed at human happiness, surely. If right living is not richest living, then right needs to be redefined.

God's unconditional love does not demand that we change. We are loved as we are. Accepting that love, though, challenges us to value ourselves as we are valued and treasured by God. For example:

> "I'm not sure, God, that you want me around in prayer this evening. I've been a rat today."
>
> "I know."
>
> "In fact I've been a stupid rat—a mean, vindictive, selfish, and stupid rat."
>
> "Yes, I know. I still love you."
>
> "Do you! Well, thanks, but I'm not proud of me."
>
> "Nor am I where today's behavior is concerned. But I love you."
>
> "How can you? Today showed the real me. I'm a worthless rat."
>
> "If you were honest and admitted to what you long for in your innermost depths and at your best moments, you wouldn't dare say you were worthless."
>
> "Mmmm! Do you mean you see worth in me that I'm not seeing at the moment?"
>
> "I sure do. And I love you."
>
> "Well again, thanks! I need to think about that for a while."
>
> "You sure do!"

Funny thing, but is that what we mean by unconditional love?

4 THE VISION

We love God because God first loved us.
1 John 4:19

BEING LOVED IS THE MOST MARVELOUS magic of life. Our being loved by God—that God loves us—is in the Bible. It is in the Christian tradition. It is inevitably sullied by fear and superstition. How much more magical might it be, if only we let it take over our lives. Can we, each of us, accept our being utterly loved by God—and revel in it?

I cannot prove that God loves us. No theologian can. We do not prove love. We know it in our hearts, we believe it, we act on it, but we cannot prove it. Signs, yes; proof, no. If we are desperate enough to try to prove that we are loved, our relationship is in trouble.

With any faith it is ultimately the same. We do not prove; we believe. The factors involved in belief are complex. Among them is the attractiveness of the vision that faith offers. A vision of our world and ourselves as unconditionally loved by God needs to be attractive and coherent if it is to compel our belief. For Christian faith, that vision cannot come out of modern fantasy; it has to have roots in the scriptures, in the traditional experience of God, and in the incarnation of Jesus Christ. Like it or not, we decide between visions of our world, but not on whim.

RE-VISIONING CHRISTIAN FAITH. A God who loves creates what God loves. Plenty of people ask why God would create what became such a thoroughly fouled-up world as ours. An honest answer is simple: I don't know, nobody knows; those who think they know need to think further. Free will and human sin are too simple as answers. They do not explain a world of disasters and diseases and the rest. The honest answer drags along a further question: Is our fouled-up world utterly unlovable? To me and many the answer is no. Strange, but we and our world are lovable, can be loved, could be created.

If God could find us lovable and create us as we are, is there a place for original sin? Are we, as we are, what God wanted? Sin is obvious, but love forgives. "I, I am the One who blots out your transgressions for my own sake, and I will not remember your sins" (Is 43:25). Isaiah has God flatly contradict the assertion of Joyce's retreat-giver, mentioned earlier, that "God would not be God if He did not punish the transgressor." Forgiveness opens the way to salvation. Salvation is being in a right relationship with God. If we think about it, knowing we are loved by a forgiving God is the most enduring motivation for right behavior in relationship with God.

Creation leads to incarnation, the core of Christian faith. God became human; the Word was made flesh. Theologians give various reasons why the Son of God should have become the son of Mary. My own answer verges on absurdity, but it is also one that in its absurdity makes sense for me. God became one of us because of unitive passion, because a loving God longed to be one with the beloved.

The final steps in this brief re-visioning of faith are Christ's passion, death, and resurrection and the continued presence of Christ in the eucharist. It is an absurd scandal that the Son of God should have died as a criminal on a Roman cross ("Christ crucified, a stumbling block to Jews and foolishness to Gentiles" [1Cor 1:23]). But if you love human life, you don't opt out of it. In Jesus' time and place, if he stood by what he lived for—what his life meant—conflict with the political authorities was a certainty and crucifixion its outcome. Rescue or avoidance would have meant opting out of the reality of human life. Resurrection is the pledge of our future with God. The eucharist is a loving God's presence to the beloved in ways that go beyond and yet continue the incarnation. These are sentences where chapters are needed, but they will do to point toward a possible picture.

Absurd is a strong word. I use it because it describes where I find myself on these issues of faith—and I am not alone. Stumbling block and foolishness are other words for absurdity. To finish that quote from Paul: "…but to those who are the called…Christ the power of God and the wisdom of God" (1 Cor 1:24). That is the power of the vision that goes beyond absurdity. In the often cruel chaos of our world, a loving God may seem absurd. Denial does nothing for the chaos and the cruelty, except that it strips away any possible permanence of meaning. Beyond absurdity there may be meaning.

FUNDAMENTAL TO MY FAITH. For me, three decisions are primary in my faith. They come first; everything else comes after them. They come in question form:

1. Is there a God?
2. Do I survive my body?
3. Does God love me?

To all three my belief answers "Yes."

Whether there is a God is a matter of belief, not knowledge. Someone who believes in a world with God cannot escape the whisper, "Perhaps there is no God." Someone who believes in a world without God cannot escape the whisper, "Perhaps there is a God." This ruthless "perhaps" is inescapable.

When we look at our universe, the possibility that it just happened cannot be denied, even if the odds are incredibly slim. The possibility that it was created somehow cannot be denied either, even if it sometimes seems incredible. When we have said "created," we have said it all; the "somehow" is of minimum moment. I look at our world in all its wonder. With Stephen Hawking, I ponder why there should be a universe for science to describe. And I believe in a creator or sustainer God.

I believe that I survive my body, that when the worms are done there is still a "me." I can't prove it, even to my own satisfaction. I know there are others (including most in our Older Testament) who believe that when life is ended they are snuffed out like a candle, leaving even less trace. I cannot prove them wrong. But a merely physical and material existence would be ultimately meaningless for me, and I do experience a meaning in life. I do believe I survive my body.

I believe that God loves me, loves us, is primarily our lover rather than our judge. What vision attracts me to this belief? The vision recognizes the human race as lovable. Possibly no century has faced human ugliness as ours has ("an unequalled sum of death, misery, and degradation," Norman Davies, *Europe,* 1996), and yet we may still be able to recognize ourselves as lovable. The vision recognizes our physical world as worth creating. No previous time has been so fully aware of the world's disasters as we are with our television and modern media, and yet we may still recognize our world as worth creating?

THE MAGIC. Visions resist language; words are refractory tools. An experience that took the wind out of my sails points toward the vision that is so difficult to describe. I was saying to a friend that I hoped that there might be relational beings peopling worlds across our universe. She asked why. I replied that it would make the creation of our universe in all its immensity more intelligible. It would dispel that sense of human egocentricity, with us existing all alone in the vastness of an infinitely expanding universe. She looked at me and said, "Tony Campbell, if you really believed in God's passionate love, you'd realize that God loves enough to create the entire universe just for you." In that expressive Irish phrase, I was gobsmacked. My head knew she was right. But I couldn't get my insides around it; I still can't. Such love is unbelievable; I believe it is right; I still hope there are millions of other peopled worlds in our universe.

Are we passionately loved by God to that extent? I believe we are, but it beggars belief. A vision is there that I'd love to be able to describe. A vision is there that I'd love to be able to see. I believe—and stumble along in the semidark as best I can. It gives a whole new sense to Paul's "through a glass, darkly" (1 Cor 13:12). What would it mean to be loved by God to that degree? What would it mean to take that on board in our lives?

At the bottom of it there is an act of faith, the conviction that a God exists. For me, on top of that act of faith sits the conviction that God is primarily loving. None of the other possibilities canvassed in classical theology have completely satisfied me. They may sound fine in a theological treatise, but they do not carry weight for me in the world I live in. So I believe in a God and in a God who loves. The Older Testament even gives me words for it: "You are precious in my sight, and honored, and I love you" (Is 43:4).

Back, then, to basic questions: Is our world creatable and are we lovable? My answer is grounded in classical and orthodox theology: Should we think that something good is beyond God, if we creatures are able to do it? Any good we can do, God can do better. If we can perceive the lovable in another, why shouldn't God? If we can see worth in our world, for all its appallingness, why shouldn't God? And why shouldn't God have created it? For me, that's the gist of it. It can do with a little bit of filling out.

Our world. When I can ask those who have been close to the poorest and least advantaged of people, my question is, "If you were God, knowing their situation, would you create these people?" The answer—after a long pause—has been, "Yes, I would." For all the squalor, degradation, and harshness, there is a joy in life and a nobility in people that eager missionaries and hardened journalists find lovable. If we can, can't God? Is it so unthinkable to have created our world? An evolutionary world might entail risks. How many of us would want God to have held back in the face of these risks? At the heart of horror, within a Nazi concentration camp, there can be nobility beyond belief: "When they come to judgment, let all the fruits that we have borne be their forgiveness" (anon., Ravensbrück).

Ourselves. We need not stop at appearances: "so marred was his appearance" (Is 52:14). Behind appearances we can be surprised to discover people we didn't expect to find. Often there is gentleness or loveliness or a wealth of experience that was hardly hinted at externally. Do we want to deny that insight to God? We are able to love, despite appearances, despite even knowledge. We know the fragilities and faults, the weaknesses and vulnerabilities, even the meanness and bitchiness of those we love, and still we love them. And they know ours, and they love us. Surely God loves better than we do?

Our God. Can God's love be less than unconditional? Classical theology requires God's love to be perfect. Is perfect love less than unconditional? Was Shakespeare right: "love is not love/Which alters when it alteration finds/Or bends with the remover to remove" (Sonnet 116)? Should we expect less of God than unconditional love? Parents can love their children unconditionally. Should we expect less of God?

A God who so loves and does not intervene is a God of mystery. Anger, frustration, grief, and pain must be part of the image of such a God. The Older Testament does not shrink from such language. We are helpless before the pain and suffering of our world. Should we claim the mystery that God is also helpless to eliminate pain and suffering from our world? We may not experience God intervening in our day-to-day lives, but this God is not powerless either. As those who love us do, God too has the power to inspire us, challenge us, support us, encourage us, and be there with us.

Cancer: Why You? Why Me?

I think of a homeless man who died of cancer. Much of his life he had been a derelict and a drifter and, in his own view, worse than worthless. He figured his cancer was a just enough punishment from God. He had earned it, but he was not the least grateful for it. He hated himself for his homosexuality, his alcoholism, his drug addiction, what he'd done to himself and to other people, and finally his cancer; and he hated the God he believed was punishing him with the cancer.

One day at the chemotherapy clinic he was talking with a woman who was dying of breast cancer. As they talked during clinic visits over the weeks and shared details of their lives, he learned that she was one of those good people typified as "a pillar of the church," and she had been all her life. He liked her; she was a good friend. They got on well. But he was puzzled by her cancer. He could account for his; he deserved it. He did not like it, but in his own opinion he could hardly argue that he did not deserve it. But that was not her case. It was perfectly obvious that there was no way she could have "deserved" her cancer. It must have just happened. That was the best explanation he could think of: it must have just happened. It was obvious that God loved her. She was one of those people you knew God loved.

A couple of weeks passed before the equally obvious dawned on him. If her cancer "just happened," perhaps his might have just happened too.

It took a couple more weeks before he made the next connection. If his cancer, like hers, had just happened, then it was possible that it was not a punishment for the life he had led. The possibility seemed remote at first, but it was there and it had to be looked at. Gradually it began to look more real. If she had cancer and God loved her, then it had just happened to her. If he had cancer and perhaps it had just happened to him, then perhaps God could even love him.

The next link fell into place like a thunderbolt, with all the immediacy of total conviction: God loved him! It was possible. It was real. God loved him. He died six months later and he had many visitors before he died. Everyone who knew him among the homeless dropped in to see him. All the workers on the street scene paid him a visit. I'm told no one left his room without having been deeply impressed. He spoke of the power of God's love and the meaning it gave to life in a way that touched the most spiritual and the most skeptical beyond belief.

5 THE CHALLENGE

Because you are precious in my sight, and honored,
and I love you.
Isaiah 43:4

IN THE INTRODUCTION, I BEGAN WITH AN admission: "I am not sure people are taking on board the full reality of the loving God they're talking about." As I see it, there are some major aspects of the standard presentation of Christian faith that get in the way of the idea of a loving God. I believe Christian faith can be presented in ways that encourage acceptance of a loving God. Often, however, a standard presentation of faith can inhibit acceptance of a God who loves deeply and unconditionally. Re-visioning is a challenge.

OUR SINFUL WORLD. Our human world can be wonderful. Our world can also be miserable, wretched, and thoroughly sinful. But even at its worst, it may not be unlovable. This insight demands a place in Christian faith, but some residual aspects of doctrine work against it.

Open conviction of the innate goodness of human beings is a relative latecomer to the Christian scene. An unease has prevailed in faith's attitude to human life, imaged as "mourning and weeping in this valley of tears." This unease can be honest witness to the intolerable aspects of injustice and oppression, ranging from the domestic tyrant's raised eyebrow or raised fist to the secret police, torturers, and special forces of global dictators. Something is right in faith's conviction that the sinful mess we are in is not the place where we ought to be. It does not mean that we are unloved, but it can inhibit our acceptance of a God who loves deeply and unconditionally.

Theology's attention whether to the origins of life or to its end entails a risk. Both the image of a beginning where humankind *was* radically better than it is now and the image of an end where humankind *will* be radically better and enjoy perfect peace and justice—"the wolf shall live with the lamb" (Is 11:6)—are images that risk cheapening our view of the present time and devaluing us who live in it. Behind these traditional positions seems to lie the belief that God could not possibly have wanted and created a world like ours. In our world, there is too much sin and suffering. God could not possibly want it or find anything lovable in it. It has to be the result of original sin; it will become lovable in the kingdom. So the theology of a loving God goes out the window. We're second best.

We can never settle for a compromise with injustice and oppression. God's passionate love for the poor and the oppressed has to energize our struggle against the structures of poverty and oppression. Precisely in the quest for faith and in the fight against injustice we can be deeply and passionately loved by God. God's love for us need not wait until our world is just. Unutterable human anguish may desire for its oppressors the pain of separation from God, but what we might want we may not get. Justice may be satisfied by the awareness revealed to oppressors of God's love for the oppressed and God's anger at the oppression as well as by their eternal sharing in God's regret and grief. Sin in our world is obvious; beyond God's anger and grief, it can be met by God's forgiveness and God's love. A vision of faith is possible in which God loves us and sees into us deeply enough to perceive the lovable in us, even in our worst sin or our worst suffering.

Any hint that humankind might have been intended to be radically better than it is or that humankind will end up in a future situation that will be radically better than the present risks the implication that we now are second-best and that God could not have wanted this world. We are cast in the role of playing Leah to Jacob's Rachel. Says Jacob: I didn't want this one; I wanted her sister (see Gn 29:25). Love relates to us as we are, not as we were or as we might become.

OUR SALVATION. Redemption language has a lot loaded against it. Salvation—if we free it from the "Jesus saves" glibness—has richer associations by far. Radically, salvation for us is our being loved by God. We need it. We've got it. It is about putting a troubled situation right. It is about being in a right relationship with God. The idea of redemption is burdened with the overtones of buying back and repayment. Love does not demand redemption; love forgives. A loving God does not need to redeem us; a loving God forgives us. A couple of biblical passages keep coming back to me. Job to God: "If I sin,…why do you not pardon my transgression and take away my iniquity?" (Jb 7:20–21). Isaiah quoting God: "I, I am the One who blots out your transgressions for my own sake, and I will not remember your sins" (Is 43:25). Only justice insists on redemption, on repaying what is owed, paying for the fault. Love, like the father of the prodigal, moves to forgiveness.

A vision claiming that God loves us, that God's compassion is deep enough to perceive the lovable in us even in the most sordid of our suffering, and that God forgives us our transgressions is a vision that calls for a theology of salvation rather than redemption. It dawns on us, whether slowly or in a flash, that we are loved by God, that in our mess God forgives us, that despite our fragility our relationship with God is right—from God's side, always right, even if from our side sometimes only maybe. That is salvation and it is gift: God's gift to us.

Such a vision needs the incarnation and needs it badly. In such a vision the incarnation is not a means of divine redemption but an expression of divine love. God so loved the world that God entered the world and took human flesh, becoming one of us. The incarnation is, in this vision, an act of unitive love, of unitive passion. Those who love want union with those they love. God wants union with us. God became one of us. The incarnation is the unique and unsurpassable expression of God's love for us.

A belief in God's utter love is wonderfully expressed in the apocryphal Jewish book of 2 Esdras, a writing roughly contemporary with the gospel of Matthew, available in the deuterocanonical section of the NRSV. The book's thinker, a prophet Ezra, is arguing with God about human destiny: "Spare your people and have mercy on your inheritance" (8:45). God replies, "You come far short of being able to love my creation more than I love it" (8:47). We need to take this to heart. Our thinking, theology, and language must make room for such love, even if we draw a different conclusion from it!

The God of 2 Esdras shares Jesus' view in Matthew that "the gate is narrow and the road is hard that leads to life, and there are few who find it" (Mt 7:14). Ezra is told, "The Most High made this world for the sake of many, but the world to come for the sake of only a few....Many have been created, but only a few shall be saved" (8:1,3). Ezra resists various appeals to mystery and, echoing Job, protests:

> But what are mortals, that you are angry with them; or what is a corruptible race, that you are so bitter against it? For in truth there is no one among those who have been born who has not acted wickedly; among those who have existed there is no one who has not done wrong. For in this, O Lord, your righteousness and goodness will be declared, when you are merciful to those who have no store of good works. (8:34–36)

Ezra's hope is anticipated at the beginning of the Bible when God is portrayed as merciful to those who have no store of good works. In Genesis 6–9, God brings on the flood because of human wickedness (Gn 6:5); accepting the inevitability of human wickedness, God declares at the end of the flood, "nor will I ever again destroy every living creature as I have done" (Gn 8:21). Love is shown to those who have no store of good works. That such texts exist invites us to choose between such images of God: the God of the narrow gate or the God who will never again destroy.

T HE SERIOUSNESS OF HUMAN LIFE. God, in dialogue with Ezra: "You come far short of being able to love my creation more than I love it." In 2 Esdras, such love did not mean the salvation of all; for us though, it may. Then the question might surface whether, if all are to be saved, we are wasting our time being good. Selective salvation offers a guarantee for the seriousness of life. Paul writes that "the sufferings of this present time are not worth comparing with the glory about to be revealed to us" (Rm 8:18). For many, this life is too serious and its sufferings and miseries too appalling for eternal salvation not to be somehow at stake.

For many, too, fear of the apparently easy is a powerful argument against belief in a loving God, a God whose love affair with humankind will not allow for loss.* Deeply rooted, it is one of those things that make me say, "I am not sure people are taking on board the full reality of the loving God they're talking about." At least one reflection, too often neglected, safeguards for me the seriousness of life and the vision of a loving God.

---

*Theoretically, at least, it is possible that God's gamble could sometimes be lost and a human being emerge who becomes wholly unlovable. Judging, we might assassinate; loving, God might after death annihilate.

Memory is essential to our human sense of identity. When we lose our memory, we lose our sense of who we are. I do not see how memory can be overlooked in our life with God. The comforting Roman Catholic doctrine of purgatory has overtones for me of a car wash or a finishing school. The car goes in dirty and comes out clean. The person goes in a rough diamond and comes out a polished gem. But what about memory? Is it likely that with death our memories would be erased and our identities retained?

Certainly, it is Christian belief that those with God will be beatifically fulfilled. Is there any incompatibility with retaining our memory? We would know ourselves to be deeply and unconditionally loved by God and we would be aware of all that we have been, including every moment of meanness and jealousy and evil. We would remember every significant moment of our lives, for better and for worse, and at the same time we would know ourselves to be beloved of God, deeply and unconditionally loved by God. There are human analogies enough to suggest that this is possible—and possibly true.

If this is true, this life is utterly serious. What I do now, I will remember for all eternity. I will know myself to be loved by God and I will remember every moment of my life: what I have been and what I have done, the rough and the smooth, the good and the bad. It is a vision that includes both a loving God and a view of human life that could not be more serious.

INTERCESSORY PRAYER is an important element in human religious experience. It is a deeply rooted, instinctive reaction of the creature in relationship with the Creator. Prayer for help is natural and spontaneous.

People pray to God for help for themselves or others. They pray to God for the church and the world. At the same time, it is a prayer that can function as an indicator of the depth of acceptance of God's unconditional love. Do we hear a strong sense in such prayer that God loves the people praying—or the others, or the church and the world—more than they themselves do. The tone of such prayer can often be a pointer to the rootedness of belief in a God who loves us passionately and unconditionally.

Prayer to God as our helper is a commonplace of Christian faith. It can be a weather vane, showing us the way the wind is blowing in our relationship with our God. Is our prayer a sharing of our needs or others' needs with one who loves us deeply? Or is there a sense of our need to move God with the urgency of our intercession? On a tug-boat in a typhoon or in some other desperate emergency, urgent intercession is utterly natural. In more ordinary times, the style of our intercessory prayer may be a pointer to the depth of our belief that God loves us passionately and unconditionally. We don't beg those who love us.

So what do we do when we must believe and we must pray? Quite frankly, I'm not sure. We are touching on the visceral as well as the rational. Maybe the viscera are not always right; maybe the rational can be out of its league. Often the more urgent our fear or the greater our need, the more the visceral takes over. A child asks: hold me tight; make it better. Being held tight can be the most important part of making it better. What more can a mother do for a dying child? When I pray for someone or something, what I ask of myself is that I try to express my prayer in ways that do not deny God's love. So I may begin, "O God, I know you love more deeply and passionately than I can hope to," and I see where it goes from there. Or I may begin, "O God, it is because I love and I believe you love even more that I turn to you now." I do not believe my prayer is needed to move God to action. I do believe that I need to share with my God what matters so much to us both.

We can image God's help in different ways. Looking at either end of the spectrum will clarify the range as a whole. As helper, God may be understood as enabler and sustainer, one who enables us to do what lies within our power, where we might have lacked the courage, the inspiration, the imagination, and so on. Or as helper, God may be understood as provider and supplier, doing for us what we are unable to do, filling the gaps left by our own weakness and fragility. As enabler and sustainer, God travels with us along the journeys of our life. As provider and supplier, God carries us to the end of whatever our particular journey may be. The enabling and sustaining power of God can be spoken of in many ways: the power of basic trust, the power that comes from another's solidly deep commitment, the power that derives from the attraction and challenge of high ideals. God as provider and supplier is the one to whom many prayers of petition are directed: "If you choose, you can make me clean" (Mk 1:40). If God loves us unconditionally, then "if you choose" is not in question. If only it was as simple as that. But if we accept God's unconditional love, our prayer needs to mirror our acceptance.

Up against the huge Philistine, Goliath, David is usually pictured as a defenseless kid who did not have a hope unless God fought his battle for him. This picture ignores what David says about himself as a shepherd: that he was fast enough to catch up with a lion or bear robbing his flock; that he was fearless enough to rescue a lamb from the predator; that he was tough enough and with quick enough reflexes to kill the lion or bear if it turned on him (1 Sm 17:34–36). This is no defenseless kid; this is one very tough young man. The use of a sling, a regular military weapon, is lateral thinking. No ordinary footsoldier would have a hope, one-on-one with Goliath. A single shot from a sling while Goliath's guard is down will finish him. What David needs from God is steadiness and nerve to enable him to do what he can do very well.

The common language of a puny David against the mighty Goliath can disparage David and misrepresent the nature of the help coming from God's commitment to him. Aspects of our intercessory prayer can be a touchstone for us as to whether we are disparaging ourselves and underselling God's commitment to us and God's love for us.

In my vision of a loving God, prayer is primarily relational. It functions in much the same way that communication does in my human relationships. To be fully myself in relationship, I need to be still enough at times to know myself. So too with God. At times, in a deeply loving relationship, I need to say what I know or what I feel, so that I hear myself say it. So too with God. At times in such a relationship I find myself silent in the other's presence. So too with God; I call it contemplation. At times, in a deeply loving relationship, I need to share what is going on for me. So too with God. At times I may need to ask the other to share with me. So too with God—but trickier. Above all, it is my experience that those who love me support me, encourage me, challenge me, hang in with me, and are present to me in so many ways. So too with God. As a rule, I don't ask God to do anything that I would not ask of a good friend.

The demands of Christian faith do not stand in the way of belief in a loving God. What belief in an unconditionally loving God may demand of us is a vision of Christian faith where the reality of sin does not exclude being loved, where God's forgiveness replaces redemption, where the reality of memory gives seriousness to every moment of human life, and where our prayer is primarily relational, trusting in a God who loves.

Faith in a loving God may not be easy, but it may be unbelievably rich.

Unconditional Love and Good Behavior

I remember chairing the opening session of a series of four talks given by a New Testament specialist, entitled "Is There a Hell?" After the talk, the first question from the floor was:

> Father, I know that this is only the first of a series of four and I know that the title has a question mark at the end of it, but I have a suspicion that the answer is going to be "No, there is no hell." In that case, my question is, "Have we wasted our time all these years being good?"

It may have been tongue-in-cheek; a rumble of agreement around the audience suggested that it struck a chord. I have mulled it over since. It is worth exploring because it touches significant bases.

Is being good a waste of time or, looked at from another point of view, is being good simply a way of living that Christians adopt in order to be acceptable to God? Is faith in God's unconditional love a soft option? Is morality based on fear of God or on something vastly deeper? These are questions that cannot be ignored.

Part of an answer lies in a story. When I slip a joke into a sermon, people usually don't laugh. I'm not sure why. I've got spontaneous laughter on two occasions. Once when I said I'd be short. They laughed derisively; well, they laughed. The other occasion is when I tell this story. It is a parable about unconditional love.

Jack comes home from work one winter's evening and finds his favorite chair pulled up in front of a roaring fire, his slippers beside it, and a drink ready and on the table by his chair.

> "Hey, darling, fantastic—but what's so special? An anniversary?"
>
> "No, no anniversary. I had a day off today and I spent a quiet couple of hours just sitting and thinking and enjoying the occasional cup of perfect coffee. It happens now and again, you know, that the coffee's perfect. Anyway, I was just sitting and thinking about us and our marriage and the blessed way our love has grown steadily deeper and deeper. Quietly it grew on me that I loved you so deeply that nothing, absolutely nothing, could ever destroy the love I have for you—nothing could ever break up our love. I was glowing so deeply with happiness I just wanted us to celebrate simply and specially."

There is one thing Jack cannot say. He cannot say:

> "Jill, darling, that is fantastic and I thank you so very much. Oh darling, you cannot believe how perfect your timing is. You see, fearing for our marriage I had decided that tonight I would permanently break off the affair I've been having—and now I won't have to."

Response from the congregation has been instantaneous, a roar of laughter. Oh no, Jack; it doesn't work that way. Silly man! If Jill loves him with that depth and that commitment, there is no way he can keep up his little affair, no way he'll want to. Poor man, he may not realize it yet, but his affair is over. Lucky man to be so loved.

No bond binds more surely than that of love that knows no bounds. And so it is with God.

6 THE INCARNATION

The Word was God....And the Word
became flesh and lived among us.
John 1:1, 14

A FEW PAGES BACK, WE LOOKED AT THE
advantages of salvation language over redemption
language. Outside religious circles, redemption is
scarcely a positive term. We no longer redeem captives,
but people do redeem their belongings from pawnbro-
kers—at a price. If someone or something has "redeeming
features," the implication is that the rest is not up to
much. When we hear that someone "redeemed themselves," we know that they fouled up first. Salvation language has advantages.

Redemption language has a lot loaded against it.
Salvation—if we free it from the "Jesus saves" glibness—has richer associations by far. Radically, salvation for us is our being loved by God. We need it.

We've got it. It is about putting a troubled situation right. It is about being in a right relationship with God. The idea of redemption is burdened with the overtones of buying back and repayment. Love does not demand redemption; love forgives. A loving God does not need to redeem us; a loving God forgives us....Only justice insists on redemption, on repaying what is owed, paying for the fault. Love, like the father of the prodigal, moves to forgiveness.

What would it do to the face of Christian faith if we went a step further and put the emphasis on the incarnation (God's becoming one of us) rather than on the redemption (usually somehow associated with the price Jesus pays on our behalf)? The Nicene Creed begins with incarnation (for us and for our salvation...he became human) but moves on to cross and resurrection, traditionally understood as redemption. What would happen to the face of Christian faith if God's primary saving act was seen to be the incarnation?

Redemption language is deeply rooted in many of the ways that Christians think and pray. In the liturgy of the Roman Catholic Church, for example, the eucharistic prayers of the Roman Missal are strongly redemptive in tone. Its eucharistic prayers have Christ—acclaimed as "the Savior" God sent "to redeem us" (Eucharistic Prayer II)—open his arms on the cross "for our sake"; in this, he fulfilled God's will and "won" for God a holy people (Eucharistic Prayer II). Alternatively, the liturgy calls to mind the death God's son "endured for our salvation," "the Victim whose death has reconciled us" to God (Eucharistic Prayer III). Sacrificial language is evident:

"we offer you his body and blood, the acceptable sacrifice which brings salvation to the whole world" (Eucharistic Prayer IV).

IF BELIEF IN THE INCARNATION of Jesus Christ is a faith claim that God's love for the human race is so intense that God became one of us, the issue has to be raised whether the language of redemption shouldn't be relegated to subordinate status and be used only in contexts where it has some appropriateness. The reason for such a claim is in the quoted paragraph above: "Only justice insists on redemption, on repaying what is owed, paying for the fault. Love, like the father of the prodigal, moves to forgiveness."

If the incarnation is the ultimate expression of God's love for humankind, is there a need for redemption? Being loved is being in right relationship with God. What sort of love would place a price on overcoming estrangement? Estrangement needs to be overcome in human relationships when things have gone awry. Estrangement needs to be overcome in the human relationship with God, where things have surely gone awry. Does love overcome estrangement by paying some kind of price? If Christ's incarnation is understood as the expression of God's unconditional love, there is no need for more from God. There is need for recognition and acceptance on the human side—but no need for more from God.

Can the whole mystery of Christian faith be summed up in John's "the Word became flesh and lived among us" (Jn 1:14)?

After the incarnation, the Nicene Creed continues: "For our sake he was crucified under Pontius Pilate; he suffered, died, and was buried. On the third day he rose again...." Was it for this passion, death, and resurrection that the Son of God became son of Mary? Or are passion, death, and resurrection natural parts of the human life embraced in the incarnation, the Son of God's becoming son of Mary? If redemption has primacy, then incarnation (God's becoming human) is a means to it, a necessary step on the way to it. If incarnation has primacy, then passion, death, and resurrection are better understood as part of God's becoming human, as the consequence of Jesus' total embrace of the ordinariness of human life.

When we realize in faith that human life is a unity that involves birth, death, and resurrection, then we can recognize that the incarnation of Jesus Christ (God's embracing human life) necessarily involves—beyond Christ's birth—his death and resurrection. If death as redemptive sacrifice is necessary, its necessity must be shown. Christ's death cannot be isolated from Christ's incarnation as though human life does not necessarily have both beginning and end, birth and death. God's unconditional love can be understood, in Karl Rahner's terms, as God's "salvific will" offering "God's divinizing and forgiving self-communication." The "cause" of our salvation can be God's love for us. A wise theologian does not ask the "why" of God's love. Christ's incarnation—birth, passion, death, and resurrection—can be "the historically irreversible manifestation of God communicating himself as merciful love, which imposes itself victoriously" (see *Sacramentum Mundi*, 5/431).

SUCH AN UNDERSTANDING allows the traditional language of redemption to be reformulated in terms of an equally traditional faith in incarnation. We can take as examples the Roman Missal's Eucharistic Prayers, noted above,

Eucharistic Prayer II has Christ opening his arms on the cross "for our sake"; in this, he fulfilled God's will and "won" for God a holy people. If the cross is understood as the outcome of Christ's living our human life to the full and facing the consequences of his teaching in Judea in that time, then it is easily reformulated: Christ opened his arms on the cross, embracing our life in its bitterest dregs, for love of us, and so won over for God the hearts of a holy people.

Eucharistic Prayer III calls to mind the death God's Son "endured for our salvation," "the Victim whose death has reconciled us" to God. The language of that last phrase is more explicitly redemptive, but it is not irredeemably so. The phrase, "the Victim whose death has reconciled us" to God, does not have to mean that God needed to be reconciled to us; it can be and perhaps rightly is to be read as our human need to be reconciled to God. In that case, reformulation is within reach: the death God's Son endured for love of us, the victim whose death has revealed God's love for us and so enabled our reconciliation with God.

Eucharistic Prayer IV speaks of Christ's body and blood, the acceptable sacrifice that brings salvation to the whole world. Reformulation here is easy once we give ourselves a little latitude in the understanding of sacrifice. "No one has greater love than this, to lay down

one's life for one's friends" (Jn 15:13). If that is not sacrifice, the word has no meaning. Christ's life was laid
down for us. Reformulation, then, is easy: Christ's body
and blood, the laying down of his own life for love of
human life and for his friends, reveals to us the depths of
God's love and so brings salvation to the whole world.

In these instances, I have spoken of reformulation. It
would be childish to think that what has to be done is to
reformulate propositions so that we can seem to be saying the same thing, when in reality we are not. What I
mean by reformulation is different. It is the task of
exploring the shape of Christian faith when a primacy is
given to incarnation over redemption. If redemption-
based expressions of faith can be reformulated as incar-
nation-based and can provide a richer and more
attractive image of God, it becomes a most worthwhile
task to reshape Christian faith in terms of incarnation
rather than redemption. What these examples show is
that the expression of Christian faith can be reshaped in
this way, emphasizing Christ's incarnation as the expression of God's love for us.

IN THE ROMAN WORLD OF JESUS' TIME, if
Jesus was to live as he did, act as he did, and say what
he did, it was inevitable that he would come into
conflict with the authorities. Serious conflict with Rome
meant crucifixion, death on a cross. There were ways to
avoid such conflict, but they would have involved aban-
doning Jesus' commitment to fullness of human life. In
the terms of the gospel, there are Jesus' words, "Do you
think that I cannot appeal to my Father, and he will at
once send me more than twelve legions of angels?"

(Mt 26:53) No ordinary human being does that. In pragmatic terms, Jesus might have moderated what he was saying or simply kept a low profile away from the towns. But that would not have been a commitment to fullness of human life.

If the incarnation is the expression of God's love for human life—in its ordinariness, not in its palaces and its luxuries (Mt 11:7–9)—then Jesus had to live to the full the life that he had chosen. There could be no compromise in his language. There could be no staying away from the centers of political life. Inevitably there had to be passion and death, cross and resurrection. Jesus' resurrection is the pledge of our future with God. Were these redemptive acts, for which the incarnation was a necessary preparation? Or were these the inevitable consequences of the commitment to ordinary human life that the incarnation expressed?

For faith that claims God's unconditional love for human life, Christ's incarnation is indeed the central act in God's history with humankind. Christ's passion, death, and resurrection are vivid witness to the value God sets on the ordinariness of human living. The language of redemption has its place not in some sense of satisfying God, but rather in the sense of liberating human beings from whatever holds them back from God.

SUCH A VISION OF CHRISTIAN FAITH does justice to the overwhelming passion of God's love for us. It claims for God a depth of compassion and insight into human lives that sees the worth and lovableness that so many of us do not see. It does not burden God with the folly of wanting what was not going to happen: human beings who would not do the wrong thing. It does not portray human life as an exile from God. Such a vision makes the claim that God so values human life as to have shared it with us, to have become one of us. It does not burden God with the folly of wanting something down the track, the Kingdom, for which so many millions of human lives would be just a preparation, a stage along the way to what God really wanted.

Such a vision of Christian faith makes the ultimate claim of "Annie Oakley theology"—any good we can do, God can do better.* At our most insightful or most loving best, we can see worth and value in human life. We can love. The challenge of Christian faith is to believe that God can do better.

In such a vision, how we came on the scene is not of major importance. Some sort of creation? Yes. Some sort of evolution? Why not? What matters is that we are here, on our earth, in our now. Scripture does not tell us about the how of our origins. Science has a big picture for the moment, open to revision and more than a tad fuzzy here and there. We are stuck with the fact that we are here; Christianity is stuck with the faith that in Christ God joined us here.

In terms of incarnation, our human relationship with God is not spelled out in language of an offended God and offending humans. Rather, it is spelled out in terms of a loving God and uncomprehending, doubting humans.

---

*With acknowledgments to the musical, *Annie Get Your Gun*. The title of one of Annie's songs is "Anything You Can Do, I Can Do Better."

In terms of incarnation, our human relationship with God is not articulated adequately by reference to our unredeemed state and God's action for our redemption. Rather, it is spelled out in terms of God's longing to be united with us and our coming to realize and accept that longing.

In terms of incarnation, our human relationship with God is grounded in a faith that God sees the lovable in us, sees worth and value in us, that God loves us. Then, in the language of John's gospel: "the Word became flesh and lived among us"; in the language of the creed: for us and for our salvation God became a human being.

Many elements may block our acceptance of what incarnation implies: God's passionate love for us, so deeply vital that God became one of us. It can be blocked by doubt that there is a God. It can be blocked by doubt that we have worth enough for God to want us, for anyone to want us, for us even to want ourselves. It can be blocked by apathy. It can be blocked by skepticism. It can be blocked by incredulity. It cannot be blocked for not being big enough or bold enough.

Incarnation and Redemption

We were deerstalking. It was summer but, high in the New Zealand mountains, it was still ferociously cold. We were fed, venison chucked on an iron skillet and strong sweet black tea. A shepherd's hut kept out the wind; sheepskins on the wooden bunks might keep out the cold. The fire wouldn't die for a while yet, and it was too early for bed.

"You say you're a theologian. What do you do?"

I hadn't dared tell Jack I was an exegete; he probably would have gone silent. He was a proud man. "Exegete" is a bit of an incomprehensible tongue-twister for most people. So I'd stuck to theologian and now I was going to pay for it. "I've been struggling with the role of incarnation and redemption in the understanding of Christian faith."

"God almighty! I cull deer for a living. I don't fool around with mouthfuls."

"Well, you asked the bloody question, and struggling with incarnation and redemption is part of what I do for a living."

"If I asked the bloody question, then you give me some sort of an answer that makes sense out here in the mountains."

"I'm not sure I've got that sort of an answer, but maybe I can give you some sort of an example to explain why it's important enough for me to struggle with."

"Orright, run your example by me."

"OK, let me try. Incarnation and redemption are like this. Two couples had really good relationships going for them. Then both of the husbands...Do you mind it being the husbands, Jack?"

"None of my business; just get on with it. I need some sleep before we tramp all over these mountains in the morning."

"OK. So, quite independently, both of the husbands did something stupid that seriously loused things up for each couple. You can imagine the sort of scenario, Jack. Both wives were livid, hurt, and furiously angry.

"One wife said if he sorted out what he'd done that had fouled up their situation so thoroughly she'd forgive him and forget the whole stupid thing.

"The other wife looked at her husband and said she couldn't see why he'd done anything so idiotic. He said he was really sorry that he'd been so stupid and their whole situation was so badly messed up; he'd try and sort it out and maybe she'd forgive him. She said he really was stupid; of course he was already forgiven. She was hurt, she was angry, she was livid, but that would heal in time. As she said to him: 'You've said you're sorry and I know that's real; I accept it because I do know you well. We'll rebuild together. Of course you're forgiven. Silly man, I love you.' She added that he'd better sort things out in due course for his own sake, but not to win back her love. She loved him—and that was that.

"The first one is pretty close to what I hear called redemption. The second said she loved him, silly man, even though he'd loused things up for both of them. That's unconditional love. In my book, that's the sort of love God has for us, and God's unconditional love is better expressed in terms of Christ's incarnation than by talk of our redemption. And that's important for the way we believe God relates to us and we relate to God. Do you agree?"

Jack grunted softly, which was about as close as he'd ever allow himself to an expression of appreciation. "I prefer culling deer. But up here in the mountains and alone a lot, it's hard to ignore God. I see why you struggle with it."

We looked at the fire and we looked at each other. Bone weary, we crawled into our bunks, pulled at the sheepskins, and slept.

7 THE DIFFERENCE

Your love is better than wine.
Song of Songs 1:2

IRESIST THE IDEA THAT FAITH in an unconditionally loving God is the easy option. It isn't. As a
matter of fact, being unconditionally loved isn't an
easy option either. It sounds good. It is good—but it
isn't easy. The more I have talked with people about
accepting God's unconditional love for us, the more I
have come to realize how challenging it is. And the more
I've found people agreeing that it certainly is not an easy
option. Cardinal Basil Hume is reported as saying that it
is harder for many people to believe that God loves them
than to believe that God exists. I'm not surprised.

We need a good look at what may be involved in a
widely held approach to Christian faith (the Roman
Catholic version, at least), and at what sort of differences
are associated with the acceptance of God's unconditional
love. The "widely held approach" is what I grew up with;

it's fine as long as you don't push it. But it's what I think I'm growing away from. The theology of an unconditionally loving God is what I hope I'm growing toward.

PLAYING FIELD AS IMAGE. Probably the most helpful description for this widely held, often traditional, approach to Christian faith is faith that searches on a level playing field for its sense of God. The theology of an unconditionally loving God that I've been advocating is faith that searches for its sense of God on a tilted playing field. By a "level playing field" I mean that the metaphors for God—judge, lover, patron-cum-benefactor, and the like—are given equal value, pointing toward what can be said of God, subverting each other, constantly reminding us of the limits and inadequacy of each, the tension between them disclosing the mystery. By a "tilted playing field" I mean that priority has been given to a primary metaphor for God, to which others are subordinated. I've been arguing for priority to be given as the primary metaphor to that of God as one who unconditionally loves us.

The level playing field where all metaphors are equal—although at any given time some metaphors may be more equal than others—has the advantage of allowing us to play one off against the rest. There are times when it is advantageous to have God as a benefactor or a judge or a patron as well as a lover. Alongside its passion for truth, theology (outside the sects) has a desire to get as many into heaven as possible. Catholic casuistry has normally favored the faithful over the law, seldom the law over the faithful. Life before God can be easier with appeal to multiple metaphors. In actual living, though, the advantages of the level playing field have to be balanced against its human risk—the risk where the metaphors are contradictory, of numbing, paralyzing, even soul-destroying ambivalence.

ANALOGIES. *With a tilted playing field,* the analogy in human experience for a theology of an unconditionally loving God may be a deep and passionate relationship. I'm not talking about sexual experience, but something much more; sex is not the only realm of passion. A deep and passionate relationship speaks of total acceptance of both lover and beloved; it speaks of engagement and utter commitment to the well-being of both; it speaks of a mutual joy of presence and being. It speaks of much more. That's the challenge—and the fear. The tilted playing field puts the love first and foremost.

For the level playing field, a different experience of relationship might be sketched as analogy. It might be, but I am not going to do it. Each of us has to draw the sketch for ourselves. Drawn by others, it somehow wouldn't be right. It is a sketch of life when the spark isn't there. Living goes on satisfactorily enough, but there's no flame to the fire. Things are comfortable, but almost too easy, almost anodyne. Safe and secure, with no place for surprises. Nothing deep and passionate. Nothing nourishing for spirit and life. The painful can be evaded; priorities can be shifted. Level playing fields allow for that.

Of these two analogies, most of us are attracted to the first, the deep and passionate. But tilted playing fields are tricky. Many of us settle for the second, the safe and secure, because that's where we are, and we count ourselves lucky.

Level playing fields give players more possibilities; no single aspect or metaphor dominates.

IMPLICATIONS OF THESE DIFFERENCES. A theology of an unconditionally loving God involves a deep and passionate relationship. The playing field is tilted. Many of us settle for a different view of God and a playing field that is level. This view involves a belief in God as a benevolent being, a decent sort of a God. Certainly not a fanatic sectarian God, but an understanding God, well disposed to us creatures and forgiving of our fragility. Well disposed and able to be prodded a little by prayer. All prayer has its place. Prayer of praise and thanks, of course; also intercessory prayer where we are asking for things for ourselves or others. We can ask God for favors and we do; we may not necessarily expect to get what we ask for, but we do assume that appropriate behavior on our part will be appropriately rewarded by God. There is an aspect, therefore, of the patron or benefactor: we expect God to take care of us and to be favorably disposed toward our interests.

There may be a recognition that the scales of justice don't work out in this life; there is an expectation that they will in the next one. Not too savagely of course. We expect God to be understanding of foibles and not too strict on minor infractions. Whatever our misgivings, most of us see ourselves on the side of the angels. The comforting aspect is that evildoers will receive their deserts. We may not be very clear about who the real evildoers actually are and we may not be very clear about what happens to them, but there is this feeling that the unfairnesses of life are evened out. There is a rewarding reason for sticking close to the straight and narrow. Divine justice will catch up with those who don't.

With a level-playing-field view of God, elements of the lover, the judge, and the patron-cum-benefactor may be mixed in. The enormous practical advantage of a traditional view is that we aren't constantly challenged; we just have to be found on the side of the angels at the end of life—keeping the rules basically. We can expect God to help us along the way, which is psychologically valuable even if it doesn't always come off. We know that being good is going to bring its reward and, perhaps even more satisfying, those who don't bother about goodness will get their appropriate come-uppance in due course. Or something like that.

A tilted playing field, with priority given to an unconditionally loving God, is not quite so easy. It is not enough to be on the side of the angels at the end. It's a poor relationship if all we can say for it is that we were there at the end. A loving God affirms a relational element in faith, invites a personal involvement. If I accept God's love, I'm accepting a relationship and taking on much more than just keeping rules. I won't be able to accept love for very long without returning it. If I return that love, I will be constantly looking to the beloved rather than to the rules. What will matter is how much I love, not what the rules allow me.

Theoretically, there can be a maddening sense that others aren't bothering about it and are still being loved. Practically, the basic challenge is not about what others are doing but about us. The challenge is: accepting ourselves as utterly loved by God, how do we respond? Our achievements are not the key; we're loved for who we are, not what we do. How do we respond when it dawns on us that it is not the things we do that ultimately matter nor the dint we make on the outer world? What matters is the person each one of us is, as well as the persons each one of us affects. Who I am, and who others are because of me, is the ultimate measure of my life. Seen in the light of God's unconditional love for us—for each of us.

Today most people are not hugely bothered about imaging heaven. But we do need to image our relationship with God here and now—and the two are related. The major benefit and, at the same time, the basic flaw of a traditional portrayal is uncoupling the quality of life in heaven from the quality of life on earth. There will be degrees of happiness, but we will not be aware of the differences. A one-liter jug and a two-liter jug and a five-liter jug hold different quantities of liquid when they are full; although the quantities are different, each of the jugs is full. Each individual will be perfectly happy. Whatever the exhortation to full human living and whatever the attractions promoted, the basic goal in this view of life is to be in God's good graces at our death. In sporting terms, when the final whistle blows we want to be among the players—not ejected from the game, or in the sin-bin.

This approach diminishes the seriousness of our lives. In this approach, what matters is not how fully we live, but that we keep the important rules of the game. In sporting terms still, when that final whistle blows, we'll be there on the same field, no matter how well we played. Equally important, in this approach, all that memory holds for human life and identity will apparently be passed over. The reality of memory demands a place for regret and sorrow as well as delight and joy. To be honest, I don't see how memory can be left out in any scenario. Most basically, this approach diminishes the seriousness of God's love for us and of our response to God's love.

CHOICES TO BE MADE. Which attitude to our relationship with God is going to enrich our lives most? That is the challenge we have to face, the basic choice before us in life. What has bite for us is the question: What is the fullest way that we can live our lives? If we have tried to achieve that, then at the end we'll have no regrets. Whatever the outcome, I tried. As one wise old leader suggested for his epitaph: He did what he could with what he had.

What can we do to live our lives to the fullest? We may wish we didn't have to ask that question, but we can hardly escape it. Some people do escape it most of their lives, maybe all their lives. Too bad, but the rest of us can't; we'd be living in permanent denial, and that is scarcely enriching. We can't escape the faith questions. I've tried, God knows. I had a ten-year stint as an agnostic, but I had to realize finally that I was not taking my own self seriously. So I have to accept what my answers to those faith questions are. Yes, I do believe in a God. Yes, I do believe I survive my body. Yes, I do believe that God is unconditionally loving.

So where does that leave us? We can alter the last response to replace "unconditionally loving" with: Yes, I do believe that God is benign, kindly, and understanding.

Well disposed. All that jazz. But I know that I don't quite believe it as the whole answer. Not deep down somewhere. Reality doesn't make full sense to me if God doesn't love us passionately in the ordinariness of life. Maybe it doesn't make much sense if God does. But for me there is more sense if God loves us deeply and passionately. So, like it or not, that's where I have to be.

Creator and Creature: Made for Each Other

When picking up friends at airports, waiting for their flight to arrive, I tend to observe the other people waiting there. The diversity in people is extraordinary and it is for me a constant source of wonder to see how often a face in the crowd is matched by another from the plane. Some are placid and patient, others irritated and impatient, and others anxious about the forthcoming reunion. Will their beloved or their friend return home relaxed or stressed, ready for closeness or confirmed in distance? There are so many different faces marked by the traces of so many different fates. As arriving passengers come through the gate, almost miraculously each face finds its mate, and across a wide range of intensities the interaction of relationship is played out in each pair.

One occasion has stayed in memory. There were thirty or forty people waiting to meet this particular flight. They were the usual motley crew typical of such occasions. But one person stood out from all the rest. With the greatest tact and delicacy, I would have to say that she was unusually unshapely and one of the least favored people I have ever seen. Playing my mind-game of "mates," I wondered who she might be waiting for. Friends perhaps, or children?

As the arrivals emerged, the usual matches were made. His yuppiness coming down the walkway; oh, of course he goes with slim-and-elegantly-costumed over there. Fred here, come in from the farm today to meet someone, the stains of earth and sun marking his broad face.

Ah, there she is, coming now, sensible, capable, down-to-earth, and perfect. Oh my God, look at this Neanderthal hulk, this gorilla of a man, lumbering in ungainly fashion toward the gate. Could it be that he and poor Bertha belong together? As the possible match crossed my mind, I glanced toward her. She was on her feet and moving toward him, her face transformed. I looked to him. He'd seen her, and his face beamed with a huge smile of recognition. Their embrace was simple and eloquent. All the impressions of ugliness were totally transformed by the evident lovability that each saw in the other and the radiant warmth and joy of their greeting. Two blithe spirits.

If, against the greatest odds, we can see such beauty in each other, surely it is not beyond God to find us lovable—and so to love us. Others can do it. Who are we to deny that God can?

8 THE MYSTERY

*For the mountains may depart and the hills be
removed, but my steadfast love shall not depart
from you.*
Isaiah 54:10

MYSTERY: WHEN ARE WE SILENT and
when do we speak? There is no way to avoid
mystery in dealing with God. If we've got an
exquisitely clear picture, then somehow we've got it
exquisitely wrong. But mystery doesn't let us off the
hook. We have our lives to live, our choices to make, and
we can't put them off by appealing to mystery. The mystery of God is the context in which we have to make
most of our choices and live our lives.

An element in the mystery of God is our need to
choose among our options for our God. Not only judge
or lover. Involved surely are the God of the few, the God
of the many, and the God of all. The God of the few is
something of a selective breeder: single out the perfect

and discard the rest. The God of the many might be doing the laundry: discard what can't be salvaged and put the rest through the wash. The God of all is mysterious: loving the lot, finding the lovable in each. Most mysterious of all is that we cannot discover which of these is God; we must instead discover our decision, our choice.

Mystery stretches minds. There is a wonderful exchange in the book, *Mister God, This Is Anna* (Collins, 1974, p. 117). Anna had just been explaining to Fynn that "the bigger the difference between us and Mister God, the more Godlike Mister God became." Fynn wanted to know what this had to do with the Sunday school teacher Anna claimed "don't teach you nuffink about Mister God." So he asked and got his answer.

> Anna: "When I find out things it makes the difference bigger and Mister God gets bigger."
> Fynn: "So?"
> Anna: "Sunday school Teacher makes the difference bigger but Mister God stays the same size. She's frightened."
> Fynn: "Hey, hold on a tick. How come she makes the difference bigger and Mister God stays the same size?"

He nearly lost the answer. It was one of those real "giveaway" lines, tossed off so quietly. Anna replied, "She just makes the people littler."

That's the risk of not letting our minds be stretched by mystery. We make our lives smaller and we make God smaller—and we sell both down the river in the process.

I have a lot of the dour Scot in me and I'd rather my life wasn't a mystery. It's taken me a long time and a lot of soul-searching to realize that it is. Some of us dour Scots are not all that quick; we take a while, but we get there. For me, the major bit of mystery in me and in all of us is that elusive quality we name "spirit." I am fascinated by the realm of spirit. Art, literature, and music give access to it; mountains and oceans touch it, great trees and evocative waters whether surging or still; church, liturgy, and prayer can touch it; stillness and silence give access to it— whatever speaks to our hearts and calls to the contemplative in each of us. Intimacy and relationship touch it. Augustine touched it when he said: "You have made us for yourself, O God, and our hearts can find no rest until they rest in you." That is part of the mystery: we can reach into the realm of spirit; we cannot rest there.

GOD IS MYSTERY. Making God smaller so that we can understand God better doesn't work. So is God judge or lover or what? My father always answered those questions with: "Probably or what." On this, he'd be right if "or what" was another way of saying "mystery." One wise old Jesuit gave this advice for theology students facing exams: "Never bring the mystery in too early and always make sure there is some mystery left at the end." It's good advice.

If I bring the mystery in too early in my thinking, I may try to live my life without committing myself to a loving God or another view of God. It may not work. I'm a limited human being and I have to work with human language and human attitudes. My attitude to God and my faith in God's attitude to me are part of that. I have to choose. Or I have to recognize the choice that has somehow happened within me.

I've got to make sure there is some mystery left at the end of my thinking, otherwise I've sold God short. God is God. God is other. Whether we like it or not, God escapes our limited human categories. Mystery is not chickening out; it is facing fact.

Archaeology yields to paleontology as, beyond the Neolithic period that we know, our imagination recedes into the ages of so long ago. How many generations existed between those we might call "prehuman" and those in whom we would recognize our forebears? What was their destiny? For me, it is shrouded in mystery. It's been said that in a few more thousands of years people may look back on our generations as "early Christians." A challenging thought that underlines the mystery of human life. Most generations have thought of themselves as near the end of time. Toward its end, the Newer Testament shifted to awareness of itself as the middle of time. What if in fact we are only near the beginning! The end may be further out of reach than the beginning.

There are areas that I wrap in mystery, because I recognize them as out of reach. One of my brothers was mentally disabled, autistic I think. I believe he lived life as fully as was possible, but it was far from the rich and full life I wish he might have had. There was a Home of Compassion next to my school, caring for children with incurable birth defects. I know they were lovingly cared for, but where rich and full human life is concerned, it seems they had been sold short. I believe that God loves them and cares about them more deeply and passionately than their caregivers or their dearest ever could. I have to entrust them to the mystery of God.

A doctor in London enabled my mother to care for my disabled brother. The doctor's name was Morgenstern, "morning star." From Vienna, his twin maiden aunts were taken to the gas chambers on their eightieth birthday, victims of the Holocaust. So many millions have been victims of unthinkable inhumanity. I can only believe in the immense anger, grief, and pain of God. And that has to be mystery.

Another aspect comes under mystery: the inactivity of God. Some would consider talk of anger and grief in God as an absurdity. What's the point of pain if you have the power to change the situation? Surely God has the power. That is where I differ. Theory of an all-powerful God is one thing; experience of a noncoercive God is another. My observation says that God does not normally exercise coercive power; my conclusion is that, to all practical effect, God does not have that sort of power. Arguments can be made for God's permissive will, allowing things for whatever good reasons. I do not find myself convinced. The Older Testament has no problem with the expression of God's anger, grief, and pain. I experience God as noncoercive, nonviolent. If God is deeply loving, as well as noncoercive and nonviolent, God is going to feel anger, grief, and pain. And that too has to be mystery.

THE PRICE OF ACCEPTING an unconditionally loving God may be acceptance of the loss of an all-powerful God. The loss may be already there; its acceptance is a further step. In accepting a loving God, we may be letting go of God the Fixer. Faced with oppression, some want God's justice rather than God's love. What we want we do not always get. We may have to settle for God's anger, grief, and pain. Anger can coexist with love. No believer in God's love can be dismissive of God's anger or God's grief and pain. Is justice met by oppressors' eternal confrontation with the truth of their own selves as well as the truth of a loving God? In claiming divine justice after death, do we ask God to do for us later what we cannot do for ourselves now? My inclination is to let a future life take care of itself, but I cannot leave it there; it determines my attitude to life now. If I demand God's justice in the future, do I diminish my acceptance of God's love in the now? I do not believe that justice, whether in this life or the next, brings pain to closure. Forgiveness is not merely a charity I extend to the offender; it is also and above all a gift I offer to myself for my own healing and my wholeness. Does that make oppressors any less vicious bastards? Of course not!

Talk of forgiveness raises three questions, provocative but real. In some circumstances at least, can forgiveness—ours or God's—open the way to transformation in those who are forgiven? Are we at times challenged to accept God's power to forgive and to love? Do we want to face forever our unforgiving refusal of our own healing?

We've known, from the outset, that the idea of a loving God is not new to Christian faith. What has been argued here is the rank, or priority, to be given to God's love in our faith. Traditionally, the loss of God—"the pain of loss"—is said to be acutely felt by the lost. Equally, the loss of those who are loved would bring grief and pain to a loving God. How often do we weigh God's loss? Or does God refuse to lose, refuse to be definitively rejected within a world as uncertain as ours? Is the priority to be given to God's love paramount? Is God's love unconditional?

Human language admits to mystery but ought not indulge it with obfuscation or linguistic snake oil. Mystery does not admit of regimentation. Vision decisions cannot be imposed on others. To run two metaphors only, if there is a lot of judging and very little loving, I am ill at ease. Does such an image adequately reflect the Judeo-Christian tradition? I want to say it doesn't. If there is a little more judging than loving or a little more loving than judging, at this stage I keep my distance. I have had my say; people's priorities are theirs, not mine. If there is a lot of loving and very little judging, I am comfortable, I smile, and I trust that I too am there. As the relationship with God grows into one of unconditional love, I hope the judge may disappear altogether. When unconditional love is the context for our living, we can be sure that appropriate behavior will be its hallmark.

WHY WE SHOULD BE AS WE ARE is a question we cannot answer. That there is goodness and lovableness in us is open to our perception. That there is suffering and misery in life is evident. Why it should have to be so is mystery, without answer. Debunking the mystery improves nothing; perhaps it eases our intellectual or emotional tension.

In it all, in this moment of now, I have to make choices for my life. A colleague commented once, "When you are more at ease with the mystery of your own person, you'll be more at ease with the mystery of God." True, but I can't wait indefinitely. I am not comfortable with mystery, only stuck with it. And I'm stuck with the awareness that somewhere deep within myself I believe in an unconditionally loving God.

The Russian-American poet Joseph Brodsky is quoted as saying, "The ability to see meaning where for all intents and purposes there is none is a professional feature of the poet's calling." Even for those who are not poets, the task of theology ought to be the sheer pursuit of meaning in faith *(fides quaerens intellectum)*. Maybe the ultimate poet-theologian who can find meaning in all of us is God. Maybe it is possible for God to love us all—deeply, passionately, and unconditionally.

A mystery of stellar magnitude!

The Mystery:
It is not that God does not love
but that God does not act
and we cannot understand.

   Britain's unremitting beastliness to Ireland will always be a stain on the record of British history. Bernard Shaw did not call it "the famine" but "the starvation"—and he was right. Irish grain was carried off under guard to England, while there were corpses in Irish fields. Stalin starved the Ukraine. What Turks did to Armenians caused savage pain, theologically expressed in lines like these:

> We choose hell. You made us know it well.
> Keep paradise for the Turk.*

The Holocaust—the systematic extermination of some six million Jews organized by Nazi Germany—is so incredible a horror that it stands as the symbol of all inhumanity. On smaller or larger scale, such inhumanity can be found in the story of every continent, almost every country, from the many millions dead in Mao's China to the many thousands of homeless in refugee camps around the world. This unspeakable parade of human violence is a challenge to any faith in a loving God.

   What changes if we say that perhaps God is not in control, that responsibility for suffering should not be laid at

---

   *Vahan Tekeyan, "We Shall Say to God," quoted from V. Guroian, *Cross Currents* 41, 1991.

God's doorstep? Then we cannot seek the meaning of the Armenian genocide or the Holocaust or any other suffering in some mysterious design of God's that relates to and explains this specific tragedy. If these are not within God's control, what demands explanation is why God should have brought into existence a universe in which the vast bulk of human suffering escapes God's control. This pushes the explanation back a stage. Perhaps it does no more than that; perhaps it distances the explanation from the immediacy and harrowing poignancy of particular tragedies. Whatever the case, the explanation is still beyond our words.

While any theist explanation must be grounded ultimately in God, when our longing for an explanation has been separated from the reality of our feeling for the suffering, it is possible to speak of God as angered and grieved by what has happened. God's anger and grief will be infinitely deeper than our own. That throws us back on the impossibility of any explanation. Then at least we know something of the depths of the mystery we cannot plumb.

Perhaps more than any other, ours is a generation that has come to recognize that violence is unacceptable in personal relationships and to an increasing degree in political relationships. Not long ago, nations took for granted that disputes over frontiers, trade, and influence were settled by war. The experience of the twentieth century has brought home the stupidity of these attitudes. The glamour of war—so often hymned in the past as the supreme achievement of male honor and glory—has been shattered by the sordid uselessness of death and suffering made evident above all by the visual impact of television. On the level of personal relationships, there is an increasing awareness that violence has no place. Of course the toddler heading out on to a busy street has to be swept up into protective arms. But coercive violence, above all on the part of an abusive male, has been put under the glare of publicity and universally condemned. Violence need not be physical; a look is violence enough, if the power to back it up is there in one form or another.

The Bible has a story in 1 Kings 13 in which an Israelite king was consecrating his brand new sanctuary at Bethel. The stately splendor of the royal ceremony was spoiled by a prophet shouting condemnation. With all the decisiveness of royal power, the king pointed to the prophet and said, "Seize him."

With all the unexpectedness of biblical story, the royal arm, stretched out in its pointing gesture, froze. The king could not get his hand back. His arm was paralyzed, stuck out there, still pointing. We might expand the dialogue a little.

> King: Is this your doing?
> Prophet: Yeah.
> King: Well, unfreeze it.
> Prophet (after a stretched silence): Say please.
> King (after a muttered oath): Please.
> Prophet (smiling): Pretty please.
> King (scowling): Please, pretty please, unfreeze my arm.

And the prophet had a word with God and the arm was unfrozen.

I won't follow the story further. It gets more and more complex. But I do want to say that I have never heard of a single bully's fist being shriveled in mid-punch or a single wife-beater's arm frozen in mid-air. In the ordinary business of life I do not experience God intervening coercively. My ordinary experience forces me to accept the loss of a coercively powerful God. Mystery again.

AFTERWORD

THESE REFLECTIONS ARE ABOUT THE changing face of faith. Not a change in faith, but a changing face. We are all aware of how one and the same person can show us different faces at different times: now a glum scowl, now a beaming smile. For faith, the change is under way.

Evidence of change is today's widespread and accepted affirmation of God as loving. The metaphor of face is strong and very human. The faces of those who judge are pictured as hard and stern, of those who love as soft and radiant. A Georges Rouault painting has the caption *dura lex sed lex* (a hard law but the law); the stern judicial face painted is as hard as granite. If God is spoken of as a loving God, to have integrity the features of faith's face must have harmony. That is what these reflections are about.

If Christian faith gives priority to God's love, Christ's incarnation (God's becoming human) is the central act of God in human history. God's becoming one of us because of love for us is what energizes and motivates Christ's death and resurrection.

Christ's death and resurrection flow out of God's commitment to the ordinariness of our human lives—the "long littleness of life." In Christ, God became one of us and in love accepted all that that involved, even to death, death on a cross. Christ's incarnation is the central expression of God's unconditional love of human life. Passion and death are part of incarnation.

The origin and the destiny of human life attract attention. For our origin, it is possible within Christian faith to affirm that God took the risks of creating an evolutionary universe or an evolutionary world, risking its possible defects. Our ignorance about our origins is vast; it allows for a multiplicity of answers. Risked evolution is one of these, among many other possibilities.* For the destiny of human life, the possibility of enduring memory and therefore a commitment to enduring truth has been raised and cannot be avoided.

The seed has always been there in Christian scripture. It may be time for the full flowering to be visible in Christian faith.

---

*For some, evolution goes along with a denial of the presence of God; for others, evolution coexists with a belief in the presence of God. For the latter, the evolution of God's universe may be described as unguided, or guided, or risked. "Unguided": God creates and sustains an evolutionary universe and leaves it to its own devices. "Guided": this affirms God's creative activity, initial and continued, and allows for the presence in one form or another of this divine activity and of evolution, so that the universe is as God wills it to be. "Risked": this might affirm that God took the risk of creating an evolutionary universe, is with it in its evolution (with joy and sorrow, happiness and pain), but without controlling the process itself.

It is not surprising that God should be believed to love us unconditionally. Any good we can do, God can do better. Confronted with human wrongdoing, the argument for God's unconditional love is simple and classically traditional. Mothers can do it, fathers can do it, others can do it; who are we to deny that God can do it?

It is not surprising that many human authorities should favor belief in God as judge; it reinforces the power of those authorities. According to such belief, the right to judge has been delegated by the divine judge to the human authority. But you don't delegate love. According to such belief, the right to dispense favor has been delegated by the divine judge. But a universally loving God does not act selectively, dispensing favor. According to such belief, insistence on law and order has the approval of the divine judge. But Jesus Christ, the embodiment of a loving God, had a reputation for eating and drinking with tax collectors and sinners (Mt 11:19 and 9:10–11). The ultimate retribution can be expected from a God who judges. With a God who loves, the outcome may be the ultimate truth of each of us. To relinquish an aspect of privilege and power in moving from stick to carrot may in the short run seem unhelpful; in the long run it may prove surprisingly wise.

If God's unconditional love belongs to the face of faith, discordant features should not mar that face. Redemption, for instance, should not be understood in ways that contradict God's love: imaged as a debt or a price to be paid, pictured as the overcoming of divine alienation. Love does not insist on payment; love is not alienated from the beloved.

Redemption is liberation from a wretched plight. It can free us to see meaning in life, in the sense of seeing deeply into the values of life rather than being arrested at the level of the images we perceive or remember. It can liberate us from captivity to life's evident pain and misery by challenging us to see and value what God sees and values in us. It can set us free by removing the shackles of fear and anxiety, enabling a radically new context for human living. Redemption can liberate us from the conviction of our unlovableness before God and set us free to respond to God's unconditional love. Redemption flows on from incarnation; its expression needs to grasp God's love for us and God's longing to be one with us.

Much traditional expression sits uncomfortably alongside language of God's unconditional love. A shift of attitude will often allow the traditional to resonate again with truth and meaning. For example, the Lamb of God who "takes away the sin of the world" can be richly understood as removing all that blocks our acceptance of God's love rather than as paying off the debt of sin.

Emphasis on God's unconditional love can contribute to bridging one of Western Christianity's deepest doctrinal divides. Divine grace, so important in the language of Roman Catholic theology, can be appropriately understood in terms of the activity of God's love. Love is not earned; it is a sheer gift of grace. Justification by faith, so central to Reformation theology, can be understood as appropriately expressed in the language of acceptance in faith of God's unconditional love. Love is not proved; it is taken on faith.

Most change challenges. Acceptance of an unconditionally loving God may make sense of life; it demands bigness of faith in God. What we know of life and our world does not allow for little gods. It stretches belief to allow God to be big. We can stretch both time and space. In time, we can look at Christian faith from the viewpoint of a couple of hundred thousand years rather than the mere couple of thousand that have passed so far. In space, with more than a hundred thousand million galaxies, if only one planet per galaxy was peopled that would make for more than one hundred thousand million peopled worlds. Peopled or not, it makes God and the universe as unbelievably big as the world of subatomic physics is unbelievably small. In all of this, our faith may be that we are unconditionally loved by God in the ordinariness of our lives.

It stretches belief; but belief in nothing may be stretching it more. The absurdity of Christian faith. The even greater absurdity of anything less.

Good Friday

We proclaim Christ crucified,
a stumbling block to Jews and an absurdity to Gentiles,
but to those who are called, Jews and Greeks alike,
Christ the power of God and the wisdom of God.

1 Corinthians 1:23–24

1. Jesus

So they took Jesus; and carrying the cross by himself, he went out to what is called The Place of the Skull, which in Hebrew is called Golgotha. There they crucified him, and with him two others, one on either side, with Jesus between them. (Jn 19:16–18)

My Father, I knew it had to come to this. In the Roman Empire, in the province of Judea, preaching the good news had to come to this.

- Freedom of the individual from ritual and regulation had to bring conflict with some of the Jewish authorities.

- Preaching with power and the signs of healing and cleansing had to awaken messianic expectations in those of the people ready for religious revolt.
- With some of the Jewish authorities unhappy and elements among the Jewish people looking for revolution and the Messiah, there had to be conflict with the Romans.

Father, I could have pulled out.

- I could have backed off, taken a low profile, kept out of the main centers and away from crowds. But that would have been untrue to my mission to proclaim your unconditional love.
- I could have asked you, Father, to come to the rescue, to get me out of here, bring me home, or intervene with power. But that would have been untrue to human life.

It is the values of human life that we treasure and that I undertook to share and live to the full. That is what this is all about: our commitment to the values of ordinary humdrum human life in all its joys and suffering. For this I was born; for this I came into the world. (See Jn 18:37)

So it had to come to this. And I had to go through with it. But, Father, I did not think it would be so hard.

- Pilate who came so close to looking at reality and truth, but was too afraid to. Instead, he ordered me scourged.

- The cruelty and inhumanity of those soldiers with the crown of thorns. Their brutality mocked so much of my faith in humankind.
- Carrying of the cross up here to Calvary, the agony of the hammering and the nails, the intolerable pain now.

Father, I did not think it would be so hard.

2. Pilate

Pilate also had an inscription written and put on the cross. It read, "Jesus of Nazareth, the King of the Jews." Many of the Jews read this inscription, because the place where Jesus was crucified was near the city; and it was written in Hebrew, in Latin, and in Greek. The chief priests of the Jews said to Pilate, "Do not write, 'The King of the Jews,' but 'This man said, I am King of the Jews.'" Pilate answered, "What I have written I have written." (Jn 19:19–22)

I am troubled and disturbed by the events of the day. We dare not risk religious riots at this festival time. We need law and order.

But this man was different from your average religious fanatic. He was no zealot rabble-rouser. You could see that in his eyes: there was no hatred, no crazy staring. There was basic peace. Yes, there was fear, of course there was fear; no man faces crucifixion without fear. But there was peace there, inner integrity.

It is hard to have to sentence a good person to death, and that is what I had to do today. But a man like that—while he is a good man, doing good and with good values—a man like that upsets society. In the political climate here, he disturbs law and order.

It is a great pity to see as good a man as that die a death meant for criminals, but that's how it had to be. It is a pity it had to come to this, but there was really no other way.

3. Soldiers

When the soldiers had crucified Jesus, they took his clothes and divided them into four parts, one for each soldier. They also took his tunic; now the tunic was seamless, woven in one piece from the top. So they said to one another, "Let us not tear it, but cast lots for it to see who will get it." This was to fulfill what the scripture says,
"They divided my clothes among themselves
and for my clothing they cast lots."
And that is what the soldiers did. (Jn 19:23–25)

Well, this one is different from the usual run. This may be the first time I've ever felt that perhaps a violator of the law shouldn't be on his cross.

Yes, he did a lot of good. Do you remember the case of the centurion's kid in Capernaum.

He could be tough at times. Were any of you on duty that time he cleaned out the temple recently? That really shook up the folks in the temple precinct. Some of them were madder than hell.

Yes, it's stuff like that, that gets Pilate edgy. He's terrified of a spark igniting a popular revolt. It would not do his reputation any good back in Rome. The emperor is strong on law and order.

This Jesus was a good man. He had good ideas and good values. He did good to people. But he bucked the system. He should have laid low, kept a low profile, compromised a bit more. It's a wonder God did not rescue him. It's a pity it had to come to this.

4. **Mary, His Mother**
Meanwhile, standing near the cross of Jesus was his mother.... (Jn 19:25)

My God, my God, did it have to come to this! The agony, the sheer agony of it. The brutality, the pain, the blood, the suffering. My son, my son, what have they done to you?

Was this what the Annunciation was all about? What was it old Simeon had said, "Your own soul a sword shall pierce"? Did the old man see this coming? Was it inevitable, so inevitable? Did it have to come to this?

Why could God not rescue him? No, it was never that way. From his birth at Bethlehem, in that stable, it was always the ordinary way. And he was such a darling baby too. Those lovely, chubby little hands, with their tender clutching fingers, grew into the strong hands of a skilled carpenter. And now they are destroyed, contorted and twisted in agony around those brutal nails.

He never used his power to save himself. I remember he told me once that he had been tempted to turn stones to bread when he was hungry. But that is not the way of human life, and his passion was to live human life and live it to the full. Another time, he was up on the temple wall and was tempted to leap off and float gently down to earth, safe in the arms of angels. But that is not how human life works. That is not the ordinary dispensation of human life. And that ordinary dispensation is what he wanted.

So, it had to come to this. My God, my God, did it have to come to this? Was there no other way? My son loved the human race, loved people, loved people in general, but genuinely loved every individual person too. He never let people down. When he made a commitment, he kept it. So he could not give up on the gospel he preached, the Good News he shared. Having chosen to live human life to the full, he had to live it to the end.

But that it should be such an end! My son, my son, why have they done this to you?

5. **Mary Magdalene**
Meanwhile, standing near the cross of Jesus were his mother...and Mary Magdalene. (Jn 19:25)

How could this ever happen to so beautiful a man! Why should a man who did so much good die in such pain and agony, come to such a disgraceful end?

This was the man who told us the story of the Prodigal Son. Instead of his Father's arms around him now, his arms are nailed out there on that cross.

Oh, the agony, the agony! I remember when, just to show him how special he was and to thank him for his preaching, I anointed his head with ointment, washed his feet with my tears, and wiped his feet with my long lovely hair. And now look: spit and dust and flies and blood—oh, the pain, the pain!

Why did it have to come to this! I think he saw it coming. He spoke of my having anointed him for burial.

- Why couldn't he have stayed in Galilee? No, he was not the type to walk away.
- Why couldn't he have compromised more? No, he was gentle and reasonable. As a rule he did not seek confrontation, but he did not shirk it when it was needed.
- Why couldn't God—his Father he loved so much— why couldn't God prevent this from happening? No, no miracles! He said that. It was our life he wanted to live.
- What a passion for life he had! He loved human life, human living. He treasured its details, its precious moments. He grieved over suffering and pain more than anyone I know. But he saw a value in life that embraced even pain and suffering. He knew the monotony and frequent meanness of human living, but he loved it in its high points and its peaks, and also in its day-to-day living. He loved it. He looked deeply into human life and he saw that it was good. No wonder he is seeing this through to the end.

In that he is like his Father. They put an extraordinarily high value on human life. So he has to see it through to the end.

6. **Beloved Disciple**
When Jesus saw his mother and the disciple whom he loved standing beside her, he said to his mother,

*"Woman, here is your son." Then he said to the disciple,
"Here is your mother." And from that hour the disciple
took her into his own home.* (Jn 19:26–27)

I'm struck speechless by this whole thing. How did it
ever come to this? Even now, he thinks of Mary and
entrusts her to me. And I'm speechless with grief and
emotion. I can find no words. I can only look up at him
and nod my assent.

Is this what the Last Supper was all about? Is this what
he meant when he passed around the bread, saying it was
his body, broken for you, given up for you? Is this what
he meant when he called the final cup the cup of his
blood, shed for all, for the forgiveness of sin?

He knew this was going to happen. He was more
detached, more farsighted than the rest of us. He could
have called on his Father to bail him out, but he wouldn't.
He never used his power for himself. He never claimed
special treatment.

The others aren't here, just the women. The women
shamed me into coming. I wanted to run too, like the rest
of the Twelve. It is not so much the fear of dying; most of
us would be ready to die with him. It is more the terrible
fear of failure, the fear of being with him while he dies. Is it
all over? Is this where it ends? He did not seem to think so;
he saw this coming. So maybe it isn't the end.

There is nothing we can do except be here. There are
no words adequate to a situation like this. We can't even
mount a desperate show of force; he would not want that.
We can only be here, be with him. At times, when things
were frightening for us, sometimes he said nothing and
did nothing, but he was just there with us, supporting us

by his presence, his commitment. So now all we can do is just be here with him.

7. Jesus

After this, when Jesus knew that all was now finished, he said (in order to fulfill the scripture), "I am thirsty." A jar full of sour wine was standing there. So they put a sponge full of the wine on a branch of hyssop and held it to his mouth. When Jesus had received the wine, he said, "It is finished." (Jn 19:29–30)

My Father, my Father, it is almost over. There is a lightness in my body and a euphoria in my pain-soaked being; it must mean that the end is very near.

For a moment, I can lift my head and look out over these people gathered here, my friends and my enemies, look out over the city of Jerusalem and all of Judea and Israel, look out over the whole world.

- Father, this kind of thing happens to them. There are two criminals here, one on each side of me. Human life can end this way or in sickness and suffering.
- And yet you, Father, you treasure it and you value it, and you love every single human person.
- I understand that. I share that love. There are glimpses of the utter goodness of human living. There is a value and a preciousness that is present in human lives; it is real, despite the suffering and ugliness that can happen.

- It is to say yes to that, Father, that I had to go through with this to the end.

Father, it is finished now—and it is only just begun. It is finished for me, in terms of my human life. There are only a few moments more. It has only just begun for so many human beings yet to come.

- Will they remember me?
- Will they realize why I died, that I had to die?
- Will they understand that my life and death says to the whole world what you, Father, said through the prophet Isaiah to Israel:

You are precious in my eyes,
and honored, and I love you. (Is 43:4)

Father, it is finished—and it has only just begun.

Then he bowed his head and gave up his spirit.